LANCELOT ANDREWES

Selected Writings

Edited with an Introduction by
P.E. Hewison

W0010724

Fyfield Books

First published in 1995 by
Carcanet Press Limited
402-406 Corn Exchange Buildings
Manchester M4 3BY

Selection and introduction copyright © P.E. Hewison 1995

A CIP catalogue record for this book
is available from the British Library.
ISBN 1 85754 118 9

The publisher acknowledges financial assistance
from the Arts Council of England

Set in 10pt Palatino by Bryan Williamson, Frome
Printed and bound in England by SRP Ltd, Exeter

Funded by
THE
ARTS
COUNCIL
OF ENGLAND

Contents

Introduction

Students of the seventeenth century might suppose that the great Puritan poet John Milton and Archbishop William Laud, that hammer of the Puritans, could not possibly agree about anything. Yet they agreed about Lancelot Andrewes. Andrewes' death in 1626 inspired the seventeen-year-old Milton to write a long elegy, asserting:

> 'At te praecipue luxi, dignissime praesul,
> Wintoniaeque olim gloria magna tuae';

> (But you I lamented above all others, most worthy bishop,
> Once the supreme glory of your own Winchester).

Laud noted the death in his diary, describing Andrewes as 'the great light of the Christian world'. This appreciation continued when the publication of his *Sermons* inspired a sixteen-line poem by Richard Crashaw on Andrewes, 'Whose fair illustrious soul led his free thought / Through learning's universe'. Crashaw was to become a Roman Catholic. This ecumenical enthusiasm clearly has little to do with Andrewes' important role in formulating the nature of Anglicanism, he himself being something of a hammer of Puritans, and indeed of Papists.

These three commentators seem to be referring to his learning, his personal holiness and his writings. The learning is undoubted: when Andrewes was asked how many languages he knew, he replied that he could not remember, but he regarded himself as fluent in fifteen. The holiness is also undoubted: five hours a day, every day, in prayer. In fact the combination meant that no one could see him until the afternoon: 'He doubted they were no true Scholars, that came to speake with him before noon.' His writings, however, are a different matter: even in his own day his sermons were not always appreciated, by the end of the seventeenth century they were hopelessly unfashionable, and remained so until a famous essay by T.S. Eliot in the 1920s began a revival which does not really seem to have lasted. Yet to many he was *'Stella praedicantium* (a Star among preachers); and an Angell in the Pulpit'. There are complications in the figure of Andrewes which need to be explained.

Lancelot Andrewes was born in London, in Thames Street, Barking, in 1555, the eldest of the thirteen children of Thomas Andrewes, master mariner. Perhaps amidst the religious strife of the reign of Mary Tudor, that Christian name represented a lost ideal world to a father of an adventurous nature. It quickly emerged that the boy was extremely clever. Mr Ward, his teacher at his first school, Coopers' Free Grammar in Radcliffe, encouraged his parents to send him to Merchant Taylors' School, under the great Richard Mulcaster, whose portrait Andrewes later hung in his study. From there he proceeded to the college associated with Merchant Taylors', Pembroke, Cambridge. At both places he was a contemporary of Edmund Spenser: their shared obsession with words, with the importance of the specifically linguistic or lexical to literary effect, may not be a coincidence. Pembroke remained at the centre of Andrewes' life for some time: he became a Fellow in 1575, Treasurer in 1580 when he was also ordained, and Master from 1590 to 1605. He was in addition a Fellow of Jesus College, Oxford, from 1576, but continued to reside in Cambridge. This is slightly curious in that Andrewes already seemed to belong in Oxford rather than in a Cambridge strongly sympathetic to Puritanism, nowhere more so than at Pembroke. William Alabaster, his contemporary at Trinity College, saw in Andrewes 'a certaine mixture of all sides of religions, which by their very novelty now in Ingland do begyn to please agayne especially such men as have some affection to Catholique faith'. At least Andrewes was not unaware of Puritan hypocrisy. Aubrey tells a splendid story of how he obtained a key to the private door of a bowling green one Sunday, bursting in to discover self-styled extremist Sabbatarians at play: 'they were strangely surprised to see the entry of one that was not of the Brotherhood.' What Andrewes did establish in Cambridge was a formidable reputation in many fields, as teacher, pastor, preacher and even administrator, taking his college from near bankruptcy to considerable prosperity.

All this, and possibly the family friendship with their neighbour, Sir Francis Walsingham, brought Andrewes a London base as Vicar of St Giles, Cripplegate (where Milton was to be buried). This large parish significantly contained many courtiers' town houses and some important theatres. It was here, and through an associated post at St Paul's Cathedral, that Andrewes really established himself as one of the great preachers of the day. Among his admirers in the congregation were John Lyly and Thomas Nashe, Euphuist writers who also display a rich, linguistically dense literary style. Another aspect of Andrewes is seen in his response to the post at St Paul's, that of Canon Penitentiary. This officer was supposed to walk in an aisle of the cathedral at certain times to give 'spiritual advice' to those who needed it. Nobody had done it for years; Andrewes revived the practice. Again, if a man is to be judged by his friends, Andrewes could produce an impressive (and international) list: the antiquarians William Camden, John Selden and Francis Junius, the jurist Hugo Grotius, the classicist Daniel Heinsius and most of all the great French scholar Isaac Casaubon.

Andrewes' final rise to eminence came in the reign of James I, who valued him both for his learning and for his strong support of the Doctrine of the Divine Right of Kings. This combination was central to his appointment as a principal preacher to the court, and also to his deployment in theological controversy. In particular Andrewes spent the years 1608 to 1610 locked in combat with the Jesuit Cardinal Bellarmine, quite simply the finest theological brain in continental Europe, chiefly over the issue of Authority. The outcome is probably best seen as a hard-fought draw. What is important about Andrewes' part in this conflict, seen in such works as *Tortura Torti* (1609) and *Responsio ad apologiam Cardinalis Bellarmini* (1610), and also about a later dispute in 1618 with the French Cardinal Du Perron, is that in the process of defending Anglicanism Andrewes defined and in a sense actually helped to create it. He saw the doctrine and practice of the Church of England as rooted in a combination of Scripture, the Early Church and Reason, or as he neatly put it: 'One Canon reduced to unity by God himself, two testaments, three creeds, four general councils, five centuries.' Another great contribution to the Anglican tradition by Andrewes was his part in the 1604 Hampton Court Conference, where he was made responsible for the production of the Old Testament historical books from Genesis to II Kings for the Authorized Version of the Bible.

Ecclesiastical advancement accompanied all this. Andrewes was Bishop of Chichester 1605-09, Bishop of Ely 1609-19, Bishop of Winchester 1619-26. His consecration at the first of these took place on 3 November, causing a two days' postponement of the opening of Parliament and thus allowing the miraculous discovery of the Gunpowder Plot – always assuming you accept the official version. In 1616 Andrewes nearly became Archbishop of Canterbury, but was passed over for the compromise nonentity George Abbot. The results were naturally disastrous, especially with regard to Puritans: many people, including the Earl of Clarendon, believed that if Andrewes had been appointed, the Civil War might have been avoided. Abbot's ineptitude was symbolized in 1621 when he accidentally killed a keeper while hunting, which of course he should not have been doing anyway. Andrewes was appointed to the commission of inquiry, and his judgement is as typical of him as the incident was of Abbot: 'Brethren, be not too busie to condemn any for Uncanonicalls according to the strictness thereof, lest we render ourselves in the same condition.' Against this it is only fair to mention Andrewes' behaviour in 1613 over the notorious Essex Divorce case, perhaps the most sordid business at the most sordid court in English history. Andrewes followed the king's wishes and voted for the divorce or rather, as an enraged Abbot put it, 'among us he said nothing.' There is always an uneasy contrast between the two sides of Andrewes' world. On the one hand is his contact with a court where corruption, intrigue and lies flourished (although observers noted that his simple presence served to restrain the king's customary 'unseemly levity'). On the other hand is his famous, and rather controversial, private chapel, with its rich furnishings, its silver candlesticks, its elaborate Communion plate, its incense, its whole High Church practice, what contemporaries called 'the beauty of holiness'.

Andrewes did not long survive the king he served so loyally. James died in 1625; Andrewes on 26 September 1626. He was buried in what is now Southwark Cathedral. His ghost haunts the rectory of Cheam in Surrey, a country retreat for the Bishops of Winchester. The figure is seen only from the knees up, since the level of the floor has changed: exactly the same story is told of the haunting of St John's College, Oxford by the ghost of William Laud.

A more solid memorial of Andrewes is to be found in his works, and especially the Sermons and the Prayers. The most important Sermons are those he preached to the court of King James in the years between 1605 and 1624 on the great festivals of Christmas Day, Ash Wednesday, Easter Sunday and Whitsunday. They were usually delivered in London, at Whitehall, Greenwich or Hampton Court; but occasionally elsewhere when there might be a particular reason: that for Easter 1617, for example, was given at Durham Cathedral, and the theme was Episcopacy: the message was directed towards Scotland. Those for Christmas Day are particularly notable, and are therefore well represented in this volume: the Nativity seems to have been a theme that inspired Andrewes. (Another link to Milton might be made here, with his *Nativity Ode* of Christmas Day 1629.) Andrewes was also required to preach on days marking the delivery of James from the machinations of his enemies, 5 November (Gunpowder Plot) and 5 August (the Gowrie Conspiracy). These sermons are more political than theological (not that the distinction is always clear in this period); moreover Andrewes seems to have had his doubts about that August day in Perth. There is a story of his going down on his knees before James begging not to have to give the Gowrie Sermon, 'that he might not mock God unless the thing were true'. There has always been a question as to exactly who was conspiring against whom in the Gowrie Conspiracy. Andrewes felt no such hesitations about the Gunpowder Plot, as can be seen in his summary in the first Gunpowder Sermon (1606), which may also serve as an introduction to his style:

This should have been done: this, the danger; What was done? This the *factum fuisset*; What the *factum est*? All these were undone, and blowen over; all the undermining disappointed; all this murder, and cruelty, and desolation defeated. The mine is discovered, the snare is broken, and we are delivered. All these, the King, Queene, Prince, Nobles, Bishops, both Houses alive, all; not a haire of any of their heads perished; not so much as the smell of fire in any of their garments.

The style here is comparatively simple by Andrewes' standards, but shows the basic elements: the short, almost staccato phrases building up to a larger effect; the use of Latin phrases which are usually immediately translated; otherwise a reasonably normal English vocabulary without Latinisms; and a quirky sense of humour ('not so much as the smell...'). Commonly, however, Andrewes went much further than this. A central procedure is to take significant words from his text and subject them to minute examination, dissection and manipulation, as T.S. Eliot puts it, 'squeezing and squeezing the word until it yields a full juice of meaning which we should never have supposed any word to possess'.

An extreme example of this is to be seen in the analysis of 'Immanuel' from the text 'Behold, a virgin shall conceive, and bear a son, and shall call His name Immanuel' (Isaiah 7:14) for the 1614 Christmas Day Sermon (see pp.130-2). Indeed a kind of litmus test of the reader's attitude to Andrewes can be found in his response to the climax of the passage, where those who know Immanuel have 'Immanu-all' and those who do not are 'in Immanu-hell'. Andrewes himself was aware of the perils of this style: 'Seek not to be saved by Synecdoche,' he warned. As his own remark demonstrates, he was perfectly capable of the pithy phrase. One of his best is his reply to those enthusiasts who rejected any Church because they were directly inspired by the Holy Ghost: 'The Dove lights on no Carrion.' Again it is important to note how the combined linguistic-theological analysis is linked into a larger progressive structure which, as Eliot noted, can be compared to that of a poem. A good example of this is the passage on Flight, or the 'Hound of Heaven' theme, in the 1605 Christmas Day Sermon (see pp.126-8). The resemblance of Andrewes' style to metaphysical poetry in particular is obvious: Donne's poetry was circulating in manuscript among the members of Andrewes' congregation. His audience was also Shakespeare's audience. Yet the final justification of his style is not aesthetic but theological, or rather an intricate combination of the two. The basic device of Andrewes' style lies in making the rhetorical distinction between *figura dictionis* and *figura sententiae*, that is between the outward meaning and the inward matter of a word, and then exploring it in terms of antithesis. What antithesis is to rhetoric, paradox is to meaning. Paradox lies at the heart of Christianity: God made Man, Christ crucified and risen. Andrewes' style can be seen as an inevitable outcome of this subject. The point is best made by Andrewes himself, in a brilliant passage from the 1606 Christmas Day Sermon (see pp.128-30), in which his exploration of the paradox of the Christian religion is a perfect fusion of style and content.

Nevertheless it has to be admitted that the style is not, and has not been, to everyone's taste. Admirers might compare Andrewes to a 'jeweller polishing a diamond', others to someone 'letting off words like squibs'. George Herbert complained about this 'way of crumbling a Text', a phrase often taken up as the seventeenth century advanced and Andrewes became less in favour. Even members of his audience could be discontented: one lord (a Scot) complained to King James that Andrewes 'did play with his Text, as a Jack-an-ape does, who takes up a thing and tosses and playes with it, and then he takes up another, and playes a little with it. Here's a pretty thing and there's a pretty thing.' This attitude was reinforced by the change of taste towards a plainer style, associated in particular with the preaching of Tillotson, so that by 1683 Evelyn could complain about an old man who 'preach'd . . . much after Bp. Andrews's method, full of logical divisions, in short and broken periods, and Latin sentences, now quite out of fashion in the pulpit, which is grown into a far more profitable way, of plain and practical discourses.' Things look slightly different from a twentieth-century viewpoint. A revival of interest in metaphysical poetry and in Andrewes have gone together. Many aspects of Andrewes' sermons reflect the concerns of very different writers of our own century. This text-crumbling paradox-lover could be seen as a combination of James Joyce and G.K. Chesterton. Ultimately, his sermons represent an unwavering confrontation of the central aspects of his religion as displayed in its central texts. His power is best experienced within the context of a whole sermon such as that for Christmas Day 1622, perhaps his finest. Andrewes as a sermon writer may not possess the emotional impact of a Jeremy Taylor, or the drama (or melodrama) of Donne, but for sheer exhilaration of intellect in both style and content he is unsurpassed.

Another side of Andrewes is to be seen in the *Preces Privatae*, or Private Papers. Throughout his life, he collected, compiled and arranged material for prayers for his own personal use, written down mainly in Latin and Greek, with some in Hebrew, in a volume described by Richard Drake as 'slubbered with his pious hands, and watered with his penitential tears'. This original manuscript is now lost, but Drake, a Fellow of Pembroke College, obtained a copy of it made by his friend Samuel Wright, who was Andrewes' secretary as Bishop of Winchester. (The only other important copy extant is that given to Laud by Andrewes shortly before his death.) Drake translated his copy and published it in 1648, dedicating it to the Prince of Wales just a few months before his father's execution. The first comprehensive edition of the originals was published in 1675. Ever since a flood a versions has poured out, for unlike the Sermons, the Prayers never became unfashionable. In 1840 J.E. Newman produced a version of the Latin text; in 1844 the famous hymn-writer J.M. Neale did the same for the Greek; and in 1883 Edmund Venables combined and revised the two. This is the version used in this volume. It is extremely accurate; it is written in an appropriately, but not pastiche, Cranmerian style; and most importantly it preserves Andrewes' own layout of the words on the page, which is a critical guide to the rhythm and meaning of the prayers (and may possibly give an indication as to how his sermons were delivered). Included here are one of his *Thanksgivings*; and the Order of Daily Devotion for two days, Monday and Friday. Andrewes provided such an Order for each day of the week, always following the same six-part structure: Introduction / Commemoration, Confession, Prayer, Profession of Faith, Intercession, Praise. The 'Intercession' section is usually of particular interest, both for highly personal content and eloquence of expression. The secret of the success of the Prayers perhaps lies in Andrewes' unique combination of two traditions normally kept separate. Like his contemporaries, Cosin and Laud, he uses the Catholic tradition of piety reaching back to St Bernard of Clairvaux, highly individualistic and emotional. This approach had been rejected as too subjective by most post-Reformation writers, in favour of a more liturgical basis. Andrewes uses these liturgical sources as well, particularly Orthodox liturgies such as that of St James. The characteristic result can be seen in the intercession for Monday, where an invocation of the Catholikos merges with autobiographical detail. The universal and the personal are brought together in a manner that came to be seen as especially Anglican. As Dean Church put it, the *Preces Privatae* bring the spirit of the *Book of Common Prayer* 'from the Church to the closet'.

Andrewes' final contribution to Anglicanism has already been briefly mentioned: the Authorized Version. His fascination with language and its theological implications made him ideal for the task of deciding between versions, or deciding what was *right* in every sense, of scholarship, of doctrine and of beauty. He bears the final responsibility for the form of such celebrated passages as the Creation and Fall, Abraham and Isaac, the Exodus, David's laments for Saul and Jonathan and for Absalom, Elijah and the 'still small voice'. The fact that the Authorized Version is little read nowadays is part of a larger deprivation for which Andrewes is a useful corrective. The Church of England of twenty-five years ago is one that Andrewes would have recognized and (generally) approved of; the present one is neither. It is no coincidence that nothing of significance by or about Andrewes has been published in those last twenty-five years. Andrewes would have deplored the loss of episcopal authority, of respect for tradition, of belief in basic doctrine; but most of all he might have deplored what perhaps lies at the root of all these failures, the abandonment of a specifically religious language. The language of God has to be different; and once people cannot talk about God properly, they cannot talk about God at all. To read Lancelot Andrewes, in the sermons, in the prayers, and in the Authorized Version, is to encounter a holy, learned and complex personality; to relish a lively mind and mastery of words; but most of all to be reminded of that power of language which is essential for religious writing to be of any great value. Lancelot Andrewes, we need you.

King's College
Michaelmas, 1994   *University of Aberdeen*

Select Bibliography

Andrewes, L., *Sermons*, Ed. & Introd. G.M. Story (1967)
Blench, J.W., *Preaching in England* (1964)
Daiches, David, *The King James Version of the English Bible* (1941)
Eliot, T.S., *For Lancelot Andrewes* (1929)
Higham, Florence, *Lancelot Andrewes* (1952)
McAdoo, H.R., *The Structure of Caroline Moral Theology* (1949)
McAdoo, H.R., *The Spirit of Anglicanism* (1965)
Mitchell, W.F., *English Pulpit Oratory from Andrewes to Tillotson* (1932)
Smyth, Charles, *The Art of Preaching* (1940)
Welsby, P.A., *Lancelot Andrewes* (1958)
Williams, Charles, *James I* (1952)
Williamson, George, *The Senecan Amble* (1951)

Editorial Note

The text of the Sermons is from *Ninety-six Sermons by . . . Lancelot Andrewes*, which form the first five volumes of the complete *Works*, edited by J.P. Wilson and J. Bliss (11 vols, Oxford, 1841-54) for the Library of Anglo-Catholic Theology.

The text of the Prayers is from *The Private Devotions of Lancelot Andrewes*, edited by Edmund Venables (1883), which is a revised version of the translations from Andrewes' Greek and Latin by J.H. Newman and J.M. Neale respectively.

A Sermon

PREACHED BEFORE THE

KING'S MAJESTY, AT WHITEHALL

on Tuesday, the Twenty-Fifth of December, A.D. MDCX.
Being Christmas-Day.

Luke ii: 10, 11.

*The Angel said unto them, Be not afraid; for behold, I bring you good
   tidings of great joy, which shall be to all people.*

*That there is born unto you this day a Saviour, Which is Christ the
   Lord, in the city of David.*

[*Et dixit illis Angelus: Nolite timere: ecce enim evangelizo vobis
   gaudium magnum, quod erit omni populo:*

*Quia natus est vobis hodie Salvator, Qui est Christus Dominus in
   civitate David.*   Latin Vulg.]

[*And the Angel said unto them, Fear not: for, behold, I bring you good
   tidings of great joy, which shall be to all people.*

*For unto you is born this day, in the city of David, a Saviour, Which is
   Christ the Lord.*   Authorized Version]

There is a word in this text, and it is *hodie*, by virtue whereof this
day may seem to challenge a special property in this text, and this
text in this day. Christ was born, is true any day; but this day
Christ was born, never but today only. For of no day in the year
can it be said *hodie natus* but of this. By which word the Holy
Ghost may seem to have marked it out, and made it the peculiar
text of the day.

Then it will not be amiss, *donec cognominatur hodie*, as the Apostle speaketh, 'while it is called today,'[1] to hear it. To-morrow,
the word *hodie* will be lost; this day and not any day else it is in
season. Let us then hear it this day which we can hear no day
besides.

It is then the first report, the very first news that came, as this

---

[1] Hebrews 3:13

1

day, of that which maketh this day so high a feast; the birth of Christ.

It came by an Angel then; no man was meet to be the messenger of it. And look, how it came then so it should come still, and none but an Angel bring it, as more fit for the tongues of Angels than of men. Yet since God hath allowed sinful men to be the reporters of it at the second hand, and the news never the worse; for that good news is good news and welcome by any, though the person be but even a foul leper that brings it:[2] yet, that the meanness of the messenger offend us not, ever we are to remember this; be the party who he will that brings it, the news of Christ's birth is a message for an Angel.

This had been news for the best prince in the earth. That these *illis* here, these parties were shepherds, that this message came to them, needs not seem strange. It found none else at the time to come to; the Angel was glad to find any to tell it to, even to tell it the first he could meet withal; none were then awake, none in case to receive it but a sort of poor shepherds, and to them he told it.

Yet it fell not out amiss that shepherds they were; the news fitted them well. It well agreed to tell shepherds of the yeaning of a strange Lamb, such a Lamb as should 'take away the sins of the world';[3] such a Lamb as they might 'send to the Ruler of the world for a present',[4] *mitte Agnum Dominatori terræ* – Esay's Lamb. Or, if ye will, to tell shepherds of the birth of a Shepherd, Ezekiel's Shepherd; *Ecce suscitabo vobis Pastorem*, 'Behold, I will raise you a Shepherd;' 'the Chief Shepherd,' 'the Great Shepherd,' and 'the Good Shepherd that gave His life for His flock.'[5] And so it was not unfit news for the persons to whom it came.

For the manner; the Angel delivereth it *evangelizando*, 'church-wise', and that was a sign this place should ever be the exchange for this news. Church-wise, I say, for he doth it by a sermon, here at this verse; and then by hymn or anthem after, at the 14th verse. A sermon; the Angel himself calls it so, *evangelizo vobis*, 'I come

---

[2] 2 Kings 7:9
[3] John 1:29
[4] Isaiah 16:1

[5] Ezekiel 34:23; 1 Peter 5:4;
Hebrews 13:20; John 10:11

2

to evangelize, to preach you a gospel;' that first. And presently after he had done his sermon, there is the hymn, *Gloria in excelsis*, taken up by the choir of Heaven. An Angel makes the one; a multitude of Angels sing the other. The whole service of this day, the sermon, the anthem, by Angels, all.

Now the end of both sermon and anthem, and of the Angels in publishing it, and of the shepherds and us in hearing it, is *gaudium*, 'joy', for the benefit and honour; *gaudium magnum*, 'great joy', for the great benefit and great honour vouchsafed our nature and us this day. 'Joy' is in the text, and if joy be in the time, it is no harm. We keep the text, if we hold the time with joy, for so the Angel doth warrant us to hold it.

Of this angelical or evangelical message, or, as not I but the Angel calleth it, sermon, these two verses I have read are a part. Whereof the former is but an *ecce*, exciting them to hear it by magnifying the message as well worth their hearing, 'Be not afraid, for behold I bring you good tidings of great joy, which shall be to all people.' The latter is the very message itself, 'that there is born unto you this day a Saviour, Which is Christ the Lord, in the city of David.'

In the former are these points; 1. 'Fear not,' it is no ill news I bring you. 2. Nay, it is 'good news'. 3. Good, for it is 'news of joy'. 4. Joy, and that no ordinary but 'great joy'. 5. Not to some few, but 'to the whole people'. 6. And not *toti populo*, 'to all one people', but *omni populo*, 'to all people whatsoever'. 7. And them, not for the present, but *quod erit omni populo*, 'that is and so shall be to all, as long as there shall be any people upon earth'. And by virtue of this *quod erit*, to us here this day. *Ecce*, 'behold', such is the news I bring.

In the latter, the message itself. The sum whereof is the birth of a Child, a Child is born. Three things are proposed of Him. 1. This Child is 'a Saviour'. 2. 'A Saviour, Which is Christ'. 3. 'Christ the Lord', *Christus Dominus*. For every saviour is not Christ, nor every christ *Christus Dominus*, 'Christ the Lord, or the Lord Christ'. He is all three.

Then have we besides three circumstances, of the 1. Persons, 2. Time, and 3. Place. 1. The persons for whom all this is, twice repeated; 1. *evangelizo vobis* in the first verse, 2. *natus vobis* in the

3

second. But this I make some doubt of whether it be a circumstance or no; I rather hold it a principal part of the substance, as the word of conveyance whereby it passeth to us. And sure there is no joy either *in evangelizo* 'the message', or *natus* 'the birth' without it, without *vobis*. But if the message and the birth itself both be ours, then it is *gaudium magnum* indeed. Specially, if we add 2. the time when, not many days hence, but even this very day. And 3. the place where, that it is in no remote region far hence, but 'in the city of David', even here hard by.

And then lastly in a word; what our parts are to perform, to these two parts, 1. this day's message, and 2. this day's birth of our 'Saviour, Christ the Lord'.

'Be not afraid.' Here is a stop, that the message cannot proceed; for the sight of the messenger hath almost marred the hearing of the message. The parties to whom it comes be in such fear as they be not in case to receive it. 'They were afraid', and that 'sore afraid', as is said in the verse before, at the sight of the Angel that came with the news.

And this was not the case of these poor men only; others, and other manner of people were so, as well as they. This Gospel of St Luke is scarce begun, we are yet but a little way in the second chapter, and we have already three *noli timeres* in it; and all, as here, at the coming of an Angel. 1. 'Fear not, Zachary.' (chap. 1. 13.) So he was afraid. 2. 'Fear not, Mary.' (chap. 1. 30.) So she was afraid. 3. And now, 'Fear not' these here, that it seems to be general to fear at an Angel's appearing.

What was it? It was not the fear of an evil conscience; they were about no harm. Zachary was at Church at his office; the blessed Virgin, I doubt not, blessedly employed; these here doing their duty, 'watching over their flocks by night'; yet feared all. What should the matter be? It is a plain sign our nature is fallen from her original; Heaven and we are not in the terms we should be, not the best of us all.

Angels are the messengers of Heaven. Messengers ever come with tidings, but whether good or bad we cannot tell. Here comes an Angel with news from Heaven; what news he brings we know not, and therefore we fear because we know not. Which shews all is not well between Heaven and us, that upon every coming

4

of an Angel we promise ourselves no better news from thence, but still are afraid of the messages and messengers that come from that place.

That the message then may proceed, this fear must be removed. In a troubled water no face will well be seen, nor by a troubled mind no message received, till it be settled. To settle them then for it; no other way, no other word to begin with but *nolite timere*, 'fear not', and that is ever the Angel's beginning. Such is our infirmity, ever he must begin with these two words, *noli timere*, 'fear not'; and so he doth seven times in this Gospel.

But fear will not be cast out with a couple of words, till they see some reason to quiet them. And no better reason, than to shew they have no reason to fear. For fear is the expectation of evil, and there is no evil toward them; and so they have no reason to fear, *quod trepidaverunt timore ubi non erat timor*.[6] As if he should say, Angels have come with weeping news, as Judges 2. 1. If I were such an one, if I came with sad tidings, ye had reason, ye might fear. But now your terror groweth out of error. You are mistaken in me, I am no such Angel; I am *Angelus evangelizans*, 'an Angel with a Gospel', one that comes with no bad news. 'Fear not' then. There is no evil toward.

No evil; and that were enough for 'fear not'. But here is a farther matter; not only *privative*, 'I bring no ill', but *positive*, 'I bring you good news.' And good news is *nolite timere* and somewhat besides, that is, 'fear not' but be of good cheer. They be two degrees plainly, though one be inferred of the other. Fear no ill, there is none to fear; there is no ill, nay there is good towards. For good news is good, in that it represents the good itself to us before it come. It is but words. True – but such words made Jacob 'revive again',[7] when he was more than half dead, even the good news of Joseph's welfare. 'If I might but hear good tidings,' saith David, when his bones were broken, 'it would make me well again';[8] that Solomon said well, 'A good messenger is a good medicine.'[9]

Specially, this here which is so good as it carrieth away the

---

[6] Psalm 53:5
[7] Genesis 45:27

[8] Psalm 51:8
[9] Proverbs 13:17

5

name from the rest, to be called the Gospel or the glad tidings, as if none so glad, nay none glad at all without it. It is, saith the Apostle, *odor suavitatis*, 'a comfortable sweet savour'.[10] It is, saith the Wise Man, *dulcedo animæ, et sanitas ossium*, 'the sweetness of the soul, the very health of the bones'.[11] It is such, saith the Prophet, 'as the lips are precious, and the feet beautiful, of them that bring it,'[12] that a Saviour is born, as by Whom 'things in Heaven and things in earth,' men and Angels – which were in fear one of another – 'are set at peace, and love;'[13] and 'love casteth out fear,'[14] giveth the true *noli timere*.

Good news of joy; for of good news there are more sorts than one. Good news it had been, if it had been but *evangelizo vobis spem*, 'news of good hope'; that had been enough for *nolite timere*. This is more, it is of joy. I wot well there is a joy in hope, *Spe gaudentes*,[15] saith the Apostle; but that joy is not full, 'till the fulness of time come.'[16] Nor it is not perfect, for it is allayed somewhat with an unpleasing mixture, which is *spes differtur*, and that, as the Wise Man saith, *affligit animam*, 'hope deferred afflicteth the soul'.[17] *Gaudium spei* is nothing to *gaudium rei*; the hope *de futuro*, of a thing to come hereafter, nothing to the actual fruition of a thing present.

And indeed, this day's news it was ever *evangelium spei*, ever in the future tense before. Even the very last before this to the blessed Virgin, *Ecce concipies*, 'Thou shalt conceive'[18] – 'Shalt'. So it was yet to come. This is the first in the present tense; not, 'is to be born', 'is to be sent', 'is to come', but *natus est, missus est, venit*, 'is born', 'is sent', 'is come'. *Hodie*, even 'today' takes no time; 'in the city David', not far hence, but even hard by. This is *evangelizo gaudium*, 'this is joy indeed'.

But even in joy there be divers degrees. All are not of one size. Some there are lesser; some, as this here, *gaudium magnum*. The fire is as the fuel is, and the joy is as the matter is. There is not like joy to a shepherd when his ewe brings him a lamb, as when his

---

[10] 2 Corinthians 2:15
[11] Proverbs 16:24
[12] Isaiah 52:7
[13] Colossians 1:20
[14] 1 John 4:18

[15] Romans 12:12
[16] John 16:24; Galatians 4:4
[17] Proverbs 13:12
[18] Luke 1:31

wife brings him a son; yet that of a lamb is a joy, such as it is. But then, if that son should prove to be *princeps pastorum*, 'the chief shepherd in all the land', that were somewhat more. But then, if he should prove to be a Cyrus, or a David, a prince, then certainly it were another manner of joy, *gaudium magnum* indeed. As the matter is, so is the joy. If great the benefit, great the person, then great the joy. And here the benefit is great, none greater; as much as the saving of us all, as much as all our lives and souls are worth; therefore great. And the person great, none so great – it is the Lord Himself – therefore *primæ magnitudinis*, 'great even as He is'. Indeed so great it is, that the Prophet bids us plainly 'remember no more former things, nor regard matters of old'.[19] This passeth them all, the joy of it puts them all down; so that none of them shall once be mentioned with it. Therefore well said the Angel, *Evangelizo gaudium magnum*.

And great it may be *intensive*, in the parties themselves; yet not great *extensive*, nor extend itself to many, not be *gaudium magnum populo*. Yes, even that way also it is great; it is public joy, it is 'joy to the people'. And well fare that joy where it is merry with all. It is added purposely this, that they might not mistake when he said, *Evangelizo vobis*, 'he brought them good news'; that though he brought it them, yet not them only; it was not appropriate to them, it was common to others. They had their parts in it, but so should others have no less than they. And every good shepherd will like it the better for that, will be *pro grege* [for the flock], and still prefer the joy of the whole flock.

In other joys it falls out as Esay tells, 'multiply the nation, and ye shall not increase their joy';[20] for that which one wins another loses: but this joy, the joy of *Puer natus est nobis*, in it 'they shall all rejoice before Thee, as men make merry in harvest, and be joyful as men that divide the spoil.' 'In harvest'; and a good harvest all the country is the better for. 'At a spoil'; wherein every one hath his share. That is *gaudium populi*, and such is this. Well figured in the place of His birth, an inn, which is *domus populi*, 'open to all passengers' that will take it up; *juris publici*, 'wherein every one

---

[19] Isaiah 43:18   [20] Isaiah 9:3

hath right'. Yea, and the most common part of the inn. For though they sort themselves and have every one their several chambers, in the stable all have interest; that is common.[21] And as the place public, so is the benefit, and so is the joy public of His birth: Christmas joy right; all fare the better for this day. *Salus populi* [the safety of the people] is the best, and so is *gaudium populi* too; and every good mind will like it so much the better that all the people have their part in it.

And this were much, *toti populo*, 'to the whole people', if it were but one; but it is *omni populo*, say Theophylact and Beda, that is, 'to all people', which is a larger extent by far. And if ye speak of great joy, this is great indeed, for it is universal, it is as great as the world is great; when not the Jew only but the Gentile, nor the Gentile but the Jew, not one people but all, keep a feast. And at this word *omni populo, nec vox hominem sonat*, 'it is not man that speaketh now', whose goodness commonly when it is at the greatest extendeth no farther but to one nation; but with God it is never great, till it come to *omni populo*. 'It is but a small thing (saith He by Esay) to raise the tribes of Jacob, or to restore the decays of Israel; I will give thee a light to the Gentiles, and a salvation to the end of the world.'[22]

As we said of the inn even now the place of His birth, so say we here of the time of it. It is well set down by St Luke to have been at the description of the whole world;[23] for that was a meet time for the Saviour of the whole world to be born, 'the dew of Whose birth is of the womb of the morning'[24] – the Psalmist in passion of joy misplacing his words, the meaning is, 'His birth from the womb is as the morning dew' which watereth and refresheth the face of the whole earth; not Gideon's fleece alone, but the whole earth;[25] not one part, not the Jews only, no partition now but *utraque unum*, 'one of two';[26] nay, one of all; all recapitulate in Himself, and from Him as a centre lines of joy drawn to all, and every part of the circle.

And we may not pass by *quod erit*, 'which shall be', which not

---

[21] Luke 2:7
[22] Isaiah 49:6
[23] Luke 2:1

[24] Psalm 110:3
[25] Judges 6:37
[26] Ephesians 2:14, 1:10

only is but shall be. For by this word we hold; it is our besat tenure. Not only to all that then were – then had we been out – but that were or ever should be to the world's end. *Omni populo*, 'all people', is the latitude or extent; *quod erit*, 'that shall be', is the longitude or continuance of the joy. *Quod erit*, that it shall be a feast of joy, so long as any people shall be to hold a feast on the face of the earth. In a word, that same *evangelium æternum* that St John saw in the Angel's hand we now hear from the Angel's mouth, 'to be preached to every nation, kindred, tongue, and people',[27] that be, or shall be while the world endureth.

So, if we read *quod erit* with *omni populo*. But some read *gaudium* with *quod erit*, (*gaudium quod erit*,) and make a note of that; the joy *quod erit*, 'that is and shall be'. For commonly all our earthly joy is *gaudium quod est, et non erit*, 'that is for the present, but continueth not'; is, but shall not be, like the blaze of a brush faggot, all of a flame and out again suddenly in a moment. *Gaudium quod erit*, 'the joy that so is as it shall be still', is grounded upon the joy of this day – Christ and His Birth. Without which our joy is as the joy of men in prison, merry for a while, but within a while sentence of death to pass upon them. Without which *extrema gaudii luctus occupat*, 'the end of all our mirth will be but mourning.'[28] All joy else is, but shall not be within a while; at leastwise, *erit quando non erit*, a time shall be when it shall not be. *Sed gaudium Meum nemo tollet a vobis*, 'but My joy' – Mine, grounded on Me – 'none shall ever take from you';[29] not sickness, not death itself. Other it shall, this it shall not; but now ye shall this day, and evermore ye shall rejoice in the holy comfort of it.

And this is the magnifying of the message. 1. No evil news, 'fear not'. 2. Nay 'good', be of good cheer. 3. 'Good news of joy'. 4. 'Of great joy'. 5. 'Public joy', *toti populo*. 6. 'Universal joy', *omni populo*. 7. 'Joy to all' that are or shall be; and again, 'joy which now is, and shall be so for ever.'

Now upon all these He setteth an *ecce*, and well He may; and that is never set by the Holy Ghost but *super res magnæ entitatis*, 'upon matters of great moment'. But upon this hill, upon the top

---

[27] Revelations 14:6
[28] Proverbs 14:13
[29] John 16:22

of it that hath so many ascents, a beacon would do well. For look, how many *ecces* in the Scriptures, so many beacons; and between them, as between these, ye shall observe a good correspondence still. This *ecce* here, to the last, *Ecce concipies* of the blessed Virgin; that, to Esay's *Ecce concipiet Virgo*; that to David's *Ecce de fructu ventris tui*; that, to Abraham's *Ecce in semine tuo*; and so up, till ye come to *semen mulieris*.[30] There they first begin, and take light one from another, till they come to the *Ecce natus est hodie*, the *ecce* of all *ecces*, the last and highest of them all. And as a beacon serveth to call up and stir up men to have regard, so is this here to excite them, and in them us all, with good attention to hear and to heed these so great good tidings. And indeed, who is not excited with it? whose eye is not turned to behold this *ecce*? whose ear standeth not attent to hear this *evangelizo*? whose heart doth not muse, 'what manner of message this should be?'[31]

This it is then, *quod natus est*. The Birth of a Child, 'That there is One born this day' the cause of all this joy.

There is joy at every birth. 'Sorrow in the travail,' saith our Saviour, 'but after the delivery the anguish is no more remembered, for joy that a man is born into the world.'[32]

But the greater he is that is born, and the more beneficial his birth, the greater ado is made. And among men, because there are none greater than princes, and great things are looked for at their hands, their births are ever used to be kept with great triumph. Pharaoh's in the Old, Herod's in the New; both their *natus ests* days of feasting.[33]

Now of Him that is born here it may truly be said, *Ecce major hîc*, 'Behold a greater is born here.'[34] One, whose birth is good news even from the poorest shepherd to the richest prince upon the earth.

Who is it? Three things are said of this Child by the Angel. 1. He is 'a Saviour'. 2. 'Which is Christ'. 3. 'Christ the Lord'. Three of His titles, well and orderly inferred one of another by good consequence. We cannot miss one of them; they be necessary all.

---

[30] Luke 1:31; Isaiah 7:14;
   Psalm 132:11; Genesis 22:18, 3:15
[31] Luke 1:29

[32] John 16:21
[33] Genesis 40:20; Mark 6:21
[34] Matthew 12:42

Our method on earth is to begin with great; in Heaven they begin with good first.

First then, 'a Saviour'; that is His Name, Jesus, *Soter*; and in that Name His benefit, *Salus*, 'saving health or salvation'. Such a name as the great Orator himself saith of it, *Soter, hoc quantum est? Ita magnum est ut latino uno verbo exprimi non possit*. 'This name Saviour is so great as no one word can express the force of it.'[35]

But we are not so much to regard the *ecce* how great it is, as *gaudium* what joy is in it; that is the point we are to speak to. And for that, men may talk what they will, but sure there is no joy in the world to the joy of a man saved; no joy so great, no news so welcome, as to one ready to perish, in case of a lost man, to hear of one that will save him. In danger of perishing by sickness, to hear of one will make him well again; by sentence of the law, of one with a pardon to save his life; by enemies, of one that will rescue and set him in safety. Tell any of these, assure them but of a Saviour, it is the best news he ever heard in his life. There is joy in the name of a Saviour. And even this way, this Child is a Saviour too. *Potest hoc facere, sed hoc non est opus Ejus*, 'This He can do, but this is not His work'; a farther matter there is, a greater salvation He came for. And it may be we need not any of these; we are not presently sick, in no fear of the law, in no danger of enemies. And it may be, if we were, we fancy to ourselves to be relieved some other way. But that which He came for, that saving we need all; and none but He can help us to it. We have therefore all cause to be glad for the Birth of this Saviour.

I know not how, but when we hear of saving or mention of a Saviour, presently our mind is carried to the saving of our skin, of our temporal state, of our bodily life, and farther saving we think not of. But there is another life not to be forgotten, and greater the dangers, and the destruction there more to be feared than of this here, and it would be well sometimes we were remembered of it. Besides our skin and flesh a soul we have, and it is our better part by far, that also hath need of a Saviour; that hath her destruction out of which, that hath her destroyer from which she would

---

[35] Cicero, *In Verrem*

be saved, and those would be thought on. Indeed our chief thought and care would be for that; how to escape the wrath, how to be saved from the destruction to come, whither our sins will certainly bring us.

Sin it is will destroy us all. And to speak of a Saviour, there is no person on earth hath so much need of a Saviour as hath a sinner. Nothing so dangerous, so deadly unto us, as is the sin in our bosom; nothing from which we have so much need to be saved, whatsoever account we make of it. From it cometh upon us all the evil of this life, and from it all the evil of the life to come; in comparison whereof these here are not worth the speaking of. Above all then we need a Saviour for our souls, and from our sins; and from the everlasting destruction which sin will bring upon us in the other life, not far from us, not from him of us that thinketh it farthest off.

Then if it be good tidings to hear of a Saviour, where it is but a matter of the loss of earth, or of this life here; how then, when it cometh to the loss of Heaven, to the danger of hell, when our soul is at the stake, and the well-doing or undoing of it for ever? He that could save our souls from that destroyer – were not the birth of such an one good news trow? Is not such a Saviour worth the hearkening after? Is He not? It is then because we have not that sense of our souls and the dangers of them, that we have of our bodies; nor that fear of our ghostly enemies, nor that lively apprehension of the eternal torments of that place, and how near we are to it, nothing being betwixt us and it but this poor puff of breath which is in our nostrils. Our carnal part is quick and sensible, our spiritual is dead and dull. We have not the feeling of our sins that we have of our sickness; if we had, we would hear this news with greater cheerfulness, and hold this day of the birth of such a Saviour with joy indeed. We cannot conceive it yet, this destruction is not near enough to affect us. But *in novissimo intelligetis plane*, 'in the end,' when the destroyer shall come and we shall find the want of a Saviour, 'we shall plainly understand this',[36] and value this benefit and the joy of it as we ought, and find there is no joy in the earth to the joy of a Saviour.

---

[36] Jeremiah 30:24

'There is born a Saviour', is the first. The Angel addeth farther, 'a Saviour Which is Christ.' For, many saviours had been born, many had God sent them that at divers times had set them free from divers dangers of their enemies; Moses, from the Egyptians; Joshua, from the Canaanites; Gideon, from the Midianites; Jephtha, from the Ammonites; Sampson, from the Philistines.[37] And indeed, the whole story of the Bible is nothing else but a calendar of saviours that God from time to time still stirred them up.

But these all were but petty saviours, there was One yet behind that was worth them all. One, that 'should save His people from their sins';[38] save not their bodies for a time, but their souls for ever, which none of those saviours could do. One therefore much spoken of, wished for, and waited for, a Saviour Which was Christ. When He came they looked for great matters, as said the woman at the well's side, for He was the most famous and greatest Saviour of all.[39] And this is He, 'a Saviour Which is Christ'. He, of Whom all the promises made mention, and He the performance of them all; of Whom all the types under the Law were shadows, and He the substance of them all; of Whom all the prophecies ran, and He the fulfilling of them all; He, of Whom all those inferior saviours were the figures and forerunners, and He the accomplishment of all that in them was wanting. This is He; Jacob's 'Shiloh', Esay's 'Immanuel', Jeremy's 'Branch', Daniel's 'Messias', Zachary's *oriens ab alto*, Aggei's *desideratus cunctis gentibus*, 'the desire of all the nations' then, and now the joy of all nations, a Saviour Which is Christ.[40]

And what is meant by this term Christ? a Saviour anointed; or, as in another place it is said more agreeable to our phrase of speaking, a Saviour 'sealed' – a Saviour under God's Great Seal.[41] That is, not as those other were, saviours raised up of a sudden upon some occasion, to serve the turn for the present, and never heard of till they came; but a Saviour in God's fore-counsel resolved on, and given forth from the beginning; promised and foretold, and now signed and sent with absolute commission and

---

[37] Judges 6:11, 11:1, 15:5
[38] Matthew 1:21
[39] John 4:25

[40] Genesis 49:10; Isaiah 7:14; Jeremiah 23:5; Daniel 9:25; Zechariah 6:12; Haggai 2:7
[41] John 6:27

13

fulness of power to be the perfect and complete Saviour of all.

And to be it, *ex officio*; His office, His very profession, to be one, that all may have right to repair unto Him, and find it at His hands. Not a Saviour incidentally, as it fell out; but one, *ex professo*, anointed to that end, and by virtue of His anointing appointed, set forth, and sent into the world to exercise this function of a Saviour; not for a time, but for ever; not to the Jews, as did the rest, but even to all the ends of the earth. So runs His bill, *Venite ad Me omnes*, 'come all';[42] and, *qui ad Me venerit non ejiciam foras*, 'of them that come to Me, I will cast none out.'[43] *Servator omnium hominum*, 'the Saviour of all men',[44] and as the Samaritans said of Him, *Servator mundi*, 'the Saviour of the world',[45] of Samaritans, Jews, Gentiles; of kings, of shepherds, and all.

And there is yet more particularity in this word Christ: three offices did God from the beginning erect to save His people by; and that, by three acts – the very heathen took notice of them – 1. *Purgare*, 2. *Illuminare*, 3. *Perficere*. 1. Priests, to purge or expiate; 2. Prophets, to illuminate or direct them; 3. Kings, to set all right, and to keep all right in that perfection which this world admitteth. And all these three had their several anointings. Aaron the Priest, Elisha the Prophet, Saul the King.[46] In the Saviour Which is Christ, His will was all should meet, that nothing in Him might want to the perfecting of this work. That He might be a perfect Saviour of all, He was all. 'A Priest after the order of Melchizedek'; a Prophet to be heard when Moses should hold his peace; a King to save His people, 'Whose name should be *Jehova Justitia nostra.*' David's Priest, Moses' Prophet, Jeremy's King.[47]

And these formerly had met double, two of them in some other; Melchizedek, King and Priest; Samuel, Priest and Prophet; David, Prophet and King. Never all three but in Him alone; and so, no perfect Christ but He; but He all, and so perfect. By His Priesthood to purge, expiate, and 'save us from our sins, being a propitiation to God for them';[48] by His prophecy to illuminate and save us from the by-paths of error, 'guiding our feet in the

---

42 Matthew 11:28
43 John 6:37
44 1 Timothy 4:10
45 John 4: 42

46 Leviticus 8:12; 1 Kings 19:16; Samuel 10:1
47 Psalm 110:4; Deuteronomy 18:18
   Jeremiah 23:6
48 1 John 2:2

way of peace';[49] by His Kingdom protecting and conducting us through the miseries of this life, till He perfect us eternally by Himself in the joys of His Heavenly Kingdom. Rightly then, 'a Saviour Which is Christ'.

Now, as in the name Saviour there was, so is there likewise joy in this name Christ; and that, many ways: 1. First, that we shall hang no more in expectation, we shall be no longer, *Vincti spei*, 'Hope's prisoners'.[50] He that should come is come. The promised Saviour, the Saviour Which is Christ is now born, and when *spes* becomes *res* then our joy is full. 2. That now there is a saving office erected, One anointed to that end, a professed Saviour to Whom all may resort. We shall not be to seek, 'there is a name given under Heaven'[51] whereby we may be sure of salvation, the Name of Christ. 3. That to this our saving we have the joint consent and good-will of all parties, in this name Christ. Christ, that is, the Anointed, what Person is He? The Son, the second Person. Anointed by whom? By the Father (*Quem unxisti*)[52] the first Person. Anointed with what? With the Holy Ghost, the third Person.[53] So a concurrence of all Persons in this Name, all willing and well-pleased with the work of our salvation. 4. If we would be saved, we would be saved *unctione*, 'by oil', not by vinegar. *Et unguentum effusum Nomen ejus*; 'and His name is Christ, one that saveth by anointing.'[54] 5. And if by oil – there be hot oils – with a gentle lenitive oil. And the oil which He useth, wherewith He is anointed, is the oil of gladness. Gladness therefore must needs go with this Name. Which oil of gladness is not for Himself but for us, not for His use but for ours. So He saith Himself in His first sermon at Nazareth, upon His text out of Esay. The anointing, this oil of gladness, was upon Him to bestow it upon us, and of us; upon them especially that through a wounded conscience were troubled with the spirit of heaviness, to turn their heaviness into joy. Glad then that He is come that by His office is to save, and come with the good liking of all; to save us by oil, and that the oil of gladness.

And yet to make our joy more full the Angel addeth the third.

[49] Luke 1:79
[50] Zechariah 9:12
[51] Acts 4:12
[52] Acts 4:27
[53] Acts 10:38
[54] Song of Solomon 1:3; Isaiah 61:1; Luke 4:17-18

'A Saviour Which is Christ, Christ the Lord.' For neither is this all. He is not Christ only. We must not stay there. For the name Christ will agree, hath been, and may be imparted to others besides. Many a king in Scripture hath had the honour to carry the name of Christ, but with a difference. The king, *christus Domini*, 'the Lord's christ'; He *Christus Dominus*, 'the Lord Christ', or 'Christ the Lord'.[55] Consider then, how great this Child is, Whose anointed kings themselves are. For if they be *christi Domini*, 'the Lord's anointed'; His they are, for He is the Lord. The Lord absolute, without any addition; ye may put it to what ye will – Lord of men and Angels, Lord of Heaven and earth, and all the hosts of them, *Dominus Christorum*, and *Dominus Dominorum*, 'Lord paramount over all'.[56]

But why the Lord? Because this name of Christ will sort with men. Nay, as He is Christ, that is, anointed, He is man only. It is His name as Man, for God cannot be anointed. But He that should save us would be more than Man; and so, more than Christ. Indeed, Christ cannot save us. He that must save us must be the Lord. For 'such a Saviour it behoveth us to have,'[57] as might not begin the work of our salvation and leave it in the midst, but go through with it and make an end too, which the former saviours could not do. Formerly, ever their complaint was, that their saviours, their christs died still, and left them to seek; their kings, and priests, and prophets, dropped away still, for 'they were not suffered to endure by reason of death'.[58] But this Saviour, this Christ, because He is the Lord, 'endureth for ever, hath an everlasting Priesthood', Kingdom, and Prophecy, and so 'is able perfectly to save them that come to God by Him.'[59] This is one reason, why hither we must come at the last to Christ the Lord, and till we be at it we be not where we should. Else, our saviours will die and leave us destitute.

But the main reason is set down by Esay, *Ego sum, Ego sum*, saith God Himself, *et præter Me non est Servator*; 'It is I, I that am the Saviour, I am, and besides Me there is no Saviour;'[60] none indeed, no true Saviour but the Lord. All other are short, *Vana*

[55] Hebrews 7:4
[56] Revelations 17:14
[57] Hebrews 7:28
[58] Hebrews 7:23, 24
[59] Hebrews 7:25
[60] Isaiah 43:11

16

salus hominis, saith the Psalm, 'Man's salvation is vain,'[61] any salvation is vain if it be not the Lord's. 1. Those christs that were not the Lord could save but the body, and not one of them quicken his own soul; Christ that is the Lord can save souls and bodies, His own and others both. Those christs that were not the Lord, could save but from carnal enemies, with arms of flesh; He, from our ghostly enemies, even 'spiritual wickedness in heavenly places',[62] from Abaddon the great destroyer of the bottomless pit. 3. They that were not the Lord could save but from worldly calamities, could but prune and take off the twigs, as it were; He, from sin itself, and so plucketh it up by the roots. 4. They that were not the Lord put it off but for a time, and after it came again – temporal only. He for ever, once for all; and is become 'Author of eternal salvation'[63] to all that depend on Him. And mark that word 'eternal', for none but the Lord can work eternal salvation. 5. They all had need of a Saviour themselves, and of this Saviour; He needs none, receives of none, imparts to all, as being not a Saviour only but *Salus ipsa in abstracto*, 'Salvation itself,' as Simeon calleth Him 'of Whose fulness we all receive'.[64] To save may agree to man; to be salvation can agree to none but to Christ the Lord. To begin and to end; to save soul and body from bodily and ghostly enemies; from sin the root, and misery the branches; for a time and for ever; to be a Saviour and to be salvation itself; Christ the Lord is all this, and can do all this. Now then we are right, and never till now. 'A Saviour Which is Christ the Lord.'

But the name 'Lord' goeth yet further, not only to save us and set us free from danger, to deliver us from evil; but to state us in as good and better condition than we forfeited by our fall, or else though we were saved we should not save by the match. To make us then savers, and not savers only but gainers and that great gainers by our salvation, He doth further impart also the estate annexed of this last title, even whatsoever He is Lord of Himself. And He is 'Lord of life,' saith St Peter;[65] life then He imparts. And He is 'Lord of glory,' saith St Paul;[66] glory then He imparts. And He is Lord of joy, *intra in gaudium Domini*, 'enter into the joy of

[61] Psalm 60:11
[62] Ephesians 6:12
[63] Hebrews 5:9
[64] Luke 2:30; John 1:14
[65] Acts 3:15
[66] 1 Corinthians 2:8

17

the Lord;'[67] joy then He imparts. Life and glory and joy; and makes us lords of them, and of whatsoever is within the name and title of Lord. For having thereto a double right, 1. by inheritance as the Son,[68] 2. and by purchase as a Redeemer (for 'therefore He died and rose again, that He might be Lord of all;'),[69] contenting Himself with the former, He is well pleased to set over the latter to us, and admit us with Himself into His estate of joint-purchase of Heaven, or whatsoever He is owner of; that in right of it we may enter into the life, glory, and joy of our Lord, and so be saved and be savers, and more than savers every way. This also is in the word 'Lord', this benefit farther we have by it.

And now, if we will put together *natus* and *Servator*, *Servator* and *Christus*, *Christus* and *Dominus*, *Dominus* and *natus*; 'born and Saviour, Saviour and Christ, Christ and the Lord, the Lord and born'; take them which way you will in combination, any of the four, then have we His two natures in one Person. In *Servator*, His Godhead; none but God is, a Saviour. In *Christus*, His Manhood; God cannot be anointed, man may. In *Dominus*, His Divine again, 'the Lord from Heaven'.[70] In *Natus*, His human nature directly, born of a woman; both ever carefully joined, and to be joined together. When St Matthew had begun his Gospel thus, 'The Book of the generation of Jesus Christ the Son of David,' – one nature, His humanity; St Mark was careful to begin his thus, 'The beginning of the Gospel of Jesus Christ the Son of God,' – the other nature, His divinity. But St John he joins them, *Verbum caro factum est*, 'the Word became flesh.'[71] *Verbum*, 'the Word', there is *Dominus*; and *caro*, 'the flesh', that is *natus*.

And even this very conjunction is a new joy. For that such an one, that the Lord would condescend to be born, besides the benefit there is also matter of honour. Even that He, so great a Person, would become such as we are, would so esteem our nature as to take it upon Him – this certainly is a great dignity and exaltation of our nature, and it is matter of new joy that He would so highly value it as to assume, associate, and unite it into one

---

[67] Matthew 25:21
[68] Hebrews 1:2
[69] Romans 14:9
[70] 1 Corinthians 15:47
[71] John 1:14

Person with the Son of God. By this we see why 'a Saviour', why 'Christ', why 'the Lord'. 'A Saviour', His name of benefit whereby He is to deliver us; 'Christ', His name of office whereby He is bound to undertake it; 'the Lord', His name of power whereby He is able to effect it. We see also why Man, and why God. First, so it should be, for of right none was to make satisfaction for man but man; and in very deed none was able to give satisfaction to God but God. So that being to satisfy God for man, He was to be God and man. Secondly, so we would wish it ourselves; if we would be saved, we would be saved by one of our nature, not by any stranger. He is born, and so one of our own nature. Again, if we would be saved, we would be saved by no inferior, but by the best; He is the Lord, and so the very best of all. And so, our desire is satisfied every way.

This blessed birth of this 'Saviour Which is Christ the Lord' thus furnished in every point to save us throughly, body and soul, from sin the destruction, and Satan the destroyer of both, and that both here, and for ever – this blessed and thrice blessed birth is the substance of this day's solemnity of the Angel's message, and of our joy.

And now to the circumstances; and first of the persons, *vobis*; 'I bring you good tidings, that to you is born', &c.

We find not any word through all but there is joy in it, and yet all is suspended till we come to this one word, *vobis*; this makes up all. This word therefore we shall do well ever to look for, and when we find it to make much of it. Nothing passeth without it; it is the word of application. But for it, all the rest are loose; this girds it on, this fastens it to us, and makes it ours. But for it, we are but in their case, *Quid nobis et Tibi*, 'What have we to do with Thee?'[72] This 'Saviour Christ the Lord', in this good time and fit place, *quid ad nos?* 'what are we the better'? *Omni populo*, is somewhat too general, and the hundredth part of them shall not be benefited by Him. We would hear it in more particularity. Why *vobis*, 'for you it is', born for you. Yea, now ye say somewhat.

And twice it is repeated for failing, in either verse once. *Evangelizo vobis*, and *natus vobis*, that ye may know the message is yours,

[72] Matthew 8:29

19

and the birth is yours; therefore the message is sent to you, because the birth concerneth you. But yours they be, both.

May we then be bold to change the person, and utter it in the first which he doth in the second, and say, *nobis!* We may sure – *Puer natus est nobis*; Esay hath said it before us.[73] And thereby lieth a mystery. The Angels they say, *vobis*: the Prophets were men; men say, *nobis*. Bid the Angel say, *nobis*, he cannot – neither sing nor say it; *Angelis* he cannot, 'to Angels' (*Nusquam Angelos*);[74] but *hominibus* 'unto men', he can and doth.[75] And this is a special high prerogative; that which the Angels can neither sing nor say, we can do both.

If then He be born to us, it is to some end. Esay tells us what it is, when he expoundeth *natus* by *datus*, 'born to us' by 'given us'. Born, to be bestowed upon us. And if given us, bestowed upon us, then He is ours. Ours His benefit, His office, His power. His benefit to save us, His office to undertake us, His power to assure us. Ours, His salvation as Jesus, His anointing as Christ, His dominion as the Lord. And if He be ours, then all His are ours; *Omnia Ejus nostra sunt*;[76] His birth ours, and if His birth, all that follow His birth, ours too.

Now then, seeing He and they be ours, will it not be well done to make our entry, to take *seisin* of Him and them, and dispose them to our best benefit? And how can we do that better than as God hath offered Him to us this day that He was born for us, so we reciprocally this day that He is born offer Him again to God as the best pleasing oblation that we can offer Him. Today, as in the Temple alive for our morning oblation; and when the time cometh of His death, offer Him as on the Cross slain for our evening sacrifice. So shall we, as Bernard wisheth us, *uti Nostro in utilitatem nostram, et de Salvatore salutem operari*, 'employ, or make use of Him for our best behoof; draw His proper extract from Him, and work salvation out of this our Saviour.'[77]

Now a word only, what is to be done on our parts and that

---

[73] Isaiah 9:6
[74] Hebrews 2:16
[75] Luke 2:14

[76] Luke 15:31
[77] St Bernard, *Sermo Tertius in Adventu Domini* (Third Sermon on the Advent of the Lord)

respectively to these two points, what we are to return to them; what to this message, and what to this birth.

To the message, *Evangelizo vobis*, this we are to return; this is due to a message – to hear it. And that we do, and that is all; we come to the Sermon, we hear it, and little we do besides. But we hear it but heavily, with a faint affection, God knoweth; we hear it not as an *ecce*, as a matter of high admiration; we hear it not as *gaudium magnum*, with that alacrity and cheerfulness we should. We hear it not as *nobis*, as if it nearly touched us, but as a matter that little concerned us, it skilled not much whether we heard it or no. Many meaner things affect us more, but this should be the joyfullest hearing that we ever heard.

And shall we not likewise perform some duty to *natus est?* Yes, even to that also. And not hear of Him, and let Him alone; hear His tidings, and let Himself go.

He was 'born for us and given us', *'natus nobis* and *donatus nobis* – both go together in the Prophet. To a gift the duty that belongeth properly, is to receive it. If He be *natus nobis* and *donatus nobis*, I trust we will take order He be *acceptus a nobis*. If 'born for us, and given us', it is our part then, we can do no less than receive Him. We evacuate the gift, disgrace both the Giver and it, if we vouchsafe not to accept of it.

How is that? how shall we receive Him? who shall give Him us? That shall One That will say unto us within a while, *Accipite*, 'Take, this is My Body,' 'by the offering whereof ye are sanctified.' 'Take, this is My Blood,' by the shedding whereof ye are saved.[78] Both in the holy mysteries ordained by God as pledges to assure us, and as conduit pipes to convey into us this and all other the benefits that come by this our Saviour.

Verily, upon His memorable days, of which this is the first, we are bound to do something in memory, or remembrance of Him. What is that? Will ye know what it is? *Hoc facite,* 'Do this in remembrance of Me.'[79]

Something would be thought on 'to return Him for all His benefits,'[80] and this day for this first, the fountain of all the rest –

---

[78] Matthew 26:26-8; Hebrews 10:10   [80] Psalm 116:12
[79] Luke 22:19

21

His birth. Some thanks would be rendered Him for it. And how can we do that better than as we are taught by him that studied the point of *quid retribuam*, and resolved it thus; no way so well as by *accipiam Calicem*, 'I will take the Cup of salvation.'[81] And so do it: so, with it taken into our hands, 'give thanks to the name of the Lord'. And when better than today, *hodie*, as we are here directed? What better day than on this day, the very day He was bestowed on us? To defer Him no longer than He did us. He deferred not us at all, but as soon as He was born sent us word the same instant; and shall we defer Him to hear of us another time, and not be as ready on our part to receive Him instantly as He was on His to bestow Himself; even presently, as soon as He was born? Sure, somewhat would be done more than ordinary this day of His birth; the day itself is more than ordinary.

And let this move us. If ever there be a day of salvation, *ecce hic est dies salutis*, behold this is it when a Saviour is born unto us. If ever an accepted time, *ecce tempus acceptum*, behold, now it is, this is that time. The birth-day hath ever been a time accepted. Then, one king forgave the trespass of his servant and received him to grace.[82] Another, being pleased, was ready in his bounty to have given away the one half of his kingdom.[83] Our Saviour Christ, our Lord, on His birth-day will be no worse than they. His bounty *then* no less than theirs.

Let us then make this so accepted a time in itself twice acceptable by our accepting, which He will acceptably take at our hands. Let us honour this day with our receiving, which He hath honoured by His first giving; yielding Him evermore (but this day, the day of it, chiefly) our unfeigned hearty thanksgiving for this so good news, for this so great a gift, both of them this day vouchsafed us; in Him and for Him, Who was Himself the gift, our 'Saviour, Christ the Lord'. To Whom, with the Father, and the Holy Ghost, three Persons, one immortal, ever-living, invisible, only wise God; be all honour, glory, blessing, praise, and thanksgiving, this day and for ever.

---

[81] Psalm 116:13
[82] Genesis 40:20-21

[83] Mark 6:23

A Sermon

PREACHED BEFORE THE

KING'S MAJESTY, AT WHITEHALL

on Wednesday, the Twenty-Fifth of December, A.D. MDCXVI.
Being Christmas-Day.

Psalm lxxxv: 10, 11.

*Mercy and Truth shall meet; Righteousness and Peace shall kiss one
another.*

*Truth shall bud out of the earth; and Righteousness shall look down
from Heaven.*

*Misericordia et Veritas obviaverunt sibi; Justitia et Pax osculatæ
sunt.*

Veritas de terra orta est; et Justitia de Cœlo prospexit.

[*Mercy and Truth are met together; Righteousness and Peace have
kissed each other.*

*Truth shall spring out of the earth; and Righteousness shall look down
from Heaven.* Authorized Version]

I have here read you two verses out of this Psalm, which is one of
the Psalms selected of old by the primitive Church, and so still
retained by ours as part of our office or service of this day, as
being proper and pertinent to the matter of the feast, and so to
the feast itself. For the meeting here specified was to be at the
birth of the Messias: so saith Rabbi Moses, and other of the Jews.
Was at the birth of our Saviour: so say the Fathers with uniform
consent, and *eo nomine* [for this reason] have made this a Christmas-
day Psalm.

As his manner is, the Psalmist in it under one compriseth the
type and the truth both; by those things which befell the people
of the Jews, the Church typical, shadowing out those things
which were to befall the Antitype of it, Christ and His Church.
For, *primâ et propriâ intentione* [in its original and literal meaning],
it cannot be denied but the Psalm was first set according to the
letter upon the turning back of the captivity of Babel. But the
Prophet knew well that was not their worst captivity, nor should
be their best delivery. There was another yet behind concerned

them more, if they understood their own state aright, which was reserved to the Messias to free them from. To that he points. Even that the Apostle complains of wherein 'the soul is led away captive under sin and Satan',[1] the very true Babel indeed as which bringeth with it everlasting confusion, from which Christ, the true Zerubbabel, is to set us free – us and them both.

There is a meeting here. A meeting at a birth. A birth that did them in Heaven, Righteousness by name, good to behold. The meeting in *obviaverunt*, the birth in *orta est*, the pleasure to behold it in *prospexit de Cœlo*. *Prospexit* is to see with delight, as when we look into some pleasant prospect.

A meeting qualified, for the manner. For they do not meet and pass by, but meet and salute as friends with an *osculatæ sunt*, a sign of love begun or renewed.

This meeting is of four. Four which of themselves, *proprie loquendo* [strictly speaking], are nothing but attributes or proper-ties of the Divine nature, but are here by the Psalmist brought in and represented to us as so many personages. Personages, I say, inasmuch as they have here personal acts ascribed to them. For to meet, to kiss, to look down, are all of them acts personal. And look, how the Psalmist presents them so we treat of them, in the same terms the text doth.

At a birth, at *orta est*, these four meet here; at *orta est Veritas*, 'the birth of Truth' *de terra*, 'from the earth'. For two *ortus* there were; and this, not His *antesæcularis ortus de Cœlo*, 'His birth before all worlds from Heaven', but His *ortus de terra*, 'His tem-poral birth from the earth'.

Lastly, the birth of this birth as I may say, the effect it wrought. Of which more there are in the neighbouring verses. Here in these, besides the meeting occasioned by it, there is but one; that such a spectacle it was as it drew Righteousness itself from Heaven to look at it. Time was when Righteousness would not have done so much; not have vouchsafed a look hitherward; therefore *respexit nos Justitia* [Righteousness looks upon us] is good news. That then and ever since she has beheld the earth

[1] Romans 7:23

24

and the dwellers in it with a far more favourable regard than before. And all for this birth's sake.

And when was all this? When He that saith of Himself 'I am the Truth,'[2] – when He was born upon earth; for *orta est Veritas*, and *natus est Christus* will fall out to be one birth. What day soever that was, this meeting was upon it. And that was this day, of all the days of the year. The meeting and the day of this meeting here all one, and the birth of Christ the cause of both. So being this day's work, this day to be dealt with most properly.

Onward we have here four honours of this day, every one of the four giving it a blessing. 1. It is the day of *ortus Veritatis*, 'Truth's birth'; 2. and the same, the day of *occursus Misericordiæ*, 'the meeting here mentioned'; 3. and of *osculum Pacis*, 'the kiss here expressed'; 4. and of *prospectus Justitiæ*, 'Righteousness' gracious respect of us'. These from each of them in several. And generally, the day of reconciling them all.

Holding us to these, we are to speak of the 1. Meeting, the 2. Parties, the 3. Birth, and the 4. Effect here specified to come of it. [I.] Of this meeting in Christ; then [II.] in Christianity, not to be broken off by us but to be renewed, and specially this day.

Here is a meeting, and that is no great matter if it be no more. How many meet we as we pass to and fro daily, and how little do we regard it? But that meeting is casual.

Somewhat more there is in set meetings. It was not by hap, not *obviaverunt* simply but *obviaverunt sibi*. *Sibi* sheweth they had an intent; they came forth on both sides, not to meet any fifth person, but to meet one another.

But not every set meeting is memorable; this is. I find a Psalm here made in remembrance of it. And lightly songs be not made, but *de raro contingentibus*; not of ordinary, but of some special great meetings.

The greatness of a meeting groweth three ways. 1. By the parties who; 2. the occasion whereon; and 3. the end whereto they meet. All three are in this. The parties in the first verse, the occasion and end in the second. The occasion a birth, an occasion

[2] John 14:6

25

oft of making great persons meet; and the end that comes of it, that Righteousness, who is to be our Judge and to give the last sentence upon us, beholds us with an aspect that promises favour.

The occasion and the end we shall touch anon. Now of the parties. If the parties great, the meeting great. The conjunction of the great lights in Heaven, the interview of great States on earth, ever bodes some great matter. Who are the parties here? Four as high, as excellent attributes, as there be any in the Godhead. Or, to keep the style of the text, four as great States as any in the Court of Heaven.

These meet, and in what manner? Great states meet otherwhile in a pitched field. Not so here. This is an *obviaverunt* with an *osculatæ sunt*: they run not one at another as enemies; they run one to another, and kiss as loving friends. And that which makes it memorable indeed is, that these parties in this manner thus meet, who if all were well known were more like to turn tail than to meet. One to run from another; nay, one to run at another to encounter, rather than run one to another to embrace and kiss. Not meet at all; at least not meet thus, standing in such terms as they did.

Mercy and Peace if they two had met, or Truth and Righteousness, they two, it had not been strange. But for those that seem to be in opposition to do it, that is it – that makes this meeting marvellous in our eyes.

Will ye stay a little and take a view of the Parties? Four they are. These four, 1. Mercy, and 2. Truth, 3. Righteousness, and 4. Peace. Which quaternion at the first sight divides itself into two and two. Mercy and Peace, they two pair well; they be *collectaneæ*, as Bernard saith of them in one place, 'bed-fellows,' sleep together; *collactaneæ*, as in another place, 'sucked one milk, one breast' both.[3] And as these two, so the other two, Truth and Righteousness, seem to be of one complexion and disposition, and commonly take part together. Of these Mercy seems to favour us; and Peace no enemy to us nor to any (seeing we must speak of

---

[3] St Bernard, *Sermo Primus in Annunciationem* (First Sermon on the Annunciation)

them as of persons) mild and gentle persons both. For Righteousness I know not well what to say: *gestat gladium* [she carries a sword], and I fear *non frustra* [not in vain].[4] Nor of Truth, who is *vera* and *severa*, 'severe' too otherwhile. These I doubt are not like affected. The reason of my doubt. One of them, Righteousness, it is told here for great news, that she but 'looked down hitherwards from Heaven'. Before then she would not have done that. A great sign it is of heart-burning, when one will not do so much as look at another – not endure his sight. We cannot promise ourselves much of her. No, nor of Truth. One was so bold in a place to say, *omnis homo mendax* [every man a liar], and feared no challenge for it.[5] By that it seems all stands not well with her neither. So then two for us, two against us.

For their order. Mercy is first, and Peace last. With both ends we shall do well enough. God send us to do but so with the midst! Yet this is not amiss that they which favour us less are in the midst; hemmed in on both sides, closed about with those that wish us well; and they between us and them. On the one side, Mercy before; on the other, Peace behind.

Another; that in this double meeting Mercy sorts not herself, goes not to Righteousness; nor Righteousness to her, but to Peace. A kind of cross meeting, as it were, there is – the better hope of accord. Mercy and Righteousness have no symbolizing quality at all, no hope of them; but Truth with Mercy hath. There is Truth as well in the promise of Mercy as in the threat of Justice.

And it stands yet better between the other two, Righteousness and Peace. Melchizedek, which is by interpretation 'King of Righteousness', the same is 'King of Salem, that is, of peace'.[6] He That 'is after the order of Melchizedek',[7] King of both, like enough to set accord between them two – both of them His lieges. This for the view of the Parties.

These meet here; but what is *obviaverunt* without *osculatæ sunt*? Better let them stand in sunder still, and never meet. There seems to be two meetings implied. One *obviaverunt* without, and another with *osculatæ sunt*.

---

[4] Romans 13:4
[5] Romans 3:4

[6] Hebrews 7:2
[7] Hebrews 6:20

27

Before they met here, they were parted the one from the other. For they that meet come from divers coasts. Before this meeting they have been in divers quarters, one from the other, and not come together thus a good while.

Their distance in place grew from their distance in affection, estranged one from the other. That they meet not I will not say; but that they meet not thus, ever before. Else, what remarkable thing were there in this meeting, or worth the composing of a Psalm, if it had been familiar with them thus to meet every other, nay any other day?

How came they then asunder that it should be a marvel to see them meet? Since naturally they are not strangers, all four in the bosom of God from all eternity – attributes all four of His undivided Essence. So, not divided of themselves; not of themselves then. That they were divided, it was about us; the quarrel ours, that made them part company. Thus I gather it: if at Christ's birth they met, at Adam's fall they parted; if when Truth was born on earth they came together, when Truth perished from the earth they fell in sunder. That was when the first lie was told, and believed – and that was *nequaquam moriemini* [Ye shall not surely die][8] – by Adam, and thereby God much wronged. So that Adam's cause it was, and so ours that first divided Heaven, yea the very attributes in God we see, and so in a sort God Himself. So they parted first. It could not be said by the Apostle that Christ 'pacified all things in Heaven and in earth',[9] if there had not in Heaven been somewhat to be taken up.

For all this yet, I deny not but they might and did meet once before. But it was an *obviaverunt* without an *osculatæ sunt*; never both these till now. Out of Christ and before His birth, they met in opposition; in Christ and at His birth, did these four lights come to meet and to be in conjunction now. They met before, *obviaverunt*; but instead of *osculatæ* it was *altercatæ sunt*. While Mercy and Peace would have Adam's and our case relieved, Righteousness and Truth would by no means endure it. The plea is drawn up and reported at large by Bernard in his first Sermon

---

[8] Genesis 3:4   [9] Colossians 1:20

upon the Annunciation. Mercy began, for out of her readiness to do good she is here, she is ever foremost. Her inclination is, or rather she herself is an inclination, to pity such as are in misery, and if she can to relieve them, yea though they deserve it not. For, which is the comfort of the miserable sinner, she looks not to the party, what he is or what he hath done or deserved, but what he suffers, in how woeful and wretched a case he is. And her plea is, *nunquid in vanum?* 'What hath God made all men for nought?' 'What profit is in their blood?'[10] It will make God's enemies rejoice. Thither it will come, if God cast them clean off. What then, 'will He cast them off for ever, will He be no more entreated? Hath God forgotten to be gracious?'[11] With these and such like *pii susurri* [holy whispers], as he calls them, did she enter into God's bowels, and make them yearn and melt into compassion. And certainly, if there were none to stand against us, there were hope Mercy had prevailed.

But Truth must be heard too, and she lays in just matter of exception; pleads, *Deus erat Verbum*; what is God but His Word?[12] and His word was – as to Adam, *morte morieris*, so to his sons, *anima quæ peccaverit*, 'the soul that sinneth that soul shall die.'[13] God may not falsify His word; His word is the truth.[14] Falsify the truth? That may not be.

And then steps up Righteousness and seconds her. That God as He is 'true in His word', so is He 'righteous in all His works'.[15] So, to *reddere suum cuique*, 'to render each his own,' to every one that is his due; and so to the sinner, *stipendium peccati*, 'the wages of sin,' that is 'death.'[16] God forbid, the Judge of the world should judge unjustly! That were, as before to make truth false, so here to do right wrong.

Nay, it went farther, and they made it their own cases. What shall become of me, said Righteousness? What use of justice if God will do no justice, if He spare sinners? And what use of me, saith Mercy, if He spare them not? Hard hold there was, inasmuch

---

[10] Psalms 89:47; 30:9
[11] Psalm 77:7, 9
[12] John 1:1
[13] Genesis 2:17

[14] Ezekiel 18:20
[15] Psalm 145:17
[16] Romans 2:6; 6:23

as *perii nisi homo moriatur*, said Righteousness, 'I die, if he die not.' And *perii, nisi misericordiam consequatur*, said Mercy, 'if he die I die too.' To this it came; and in those terms brake up the meeting, and away they went one from the other. Truth went into exile, as a stranger upon earth: – *Terras Astræa reliquit*,[17] she confined herself in Heaven, where so aliened she was as she would not so much as look down hither upon us.

Mercy, she stayed below still. *Ubi enim Misericordia esset*, saith Hugo well, *si cum misero non esset?* 'Where should Mercy be, if with misery she should not be?'[18]

As for Peace, she went between both, to see if she could make them meet again in better terms. For without such a meeting, no good to be done for us.

For meet they must, and that in other terms, or it will go wrong with us; our salvation lies a bleeding all this while. The plea hangs, and we stand as the prisoner at the bar, and know not what shall become of us. For though two be for us, there are two against us, as strong and more stiff than they. So that much depends upon this second meeting, upon the composing or taking up this difference. For these must be at peace between themselves, before they be at peace with us, or we with God. And this is sure; we shall never meet in Heaven, if they meet no more.

And many means were made for this meeting many times, but it would not be. Where stayed it? It was not long of Mercy, she would be easily entreated to give a new meeting – no question of her. Oft did she look up to Heaven, but Righteousness would not look down. Not look? not that? small hope she would be got to meet that would not look that way-ward.

Indeed, all the question is of her. It is Truth and she that hold off, but specially she. Upon the birth you see here is no mention of any in particular but of her, as much to say as the rest might be dealt with; she only it was that stood out. And yet she must be got to meet, or else no meeting.

---

[17] Ovid, *Metamorphoses*, I.150

[18] Hugo of St Victor, *Annotationes elucidatoriæ in Psalmos* (Elucidatory Notes on the Psalms)

All the hope is, that she doth not refuse simply never to meet more, but stands upon satisfaction; else Righteousness should not be righteous. Being satisfied, then she will; remaining unsatisfied, so she will not meet.

All stands then on her satisfying; how to devise to give her satisfaction to her mind that so she may be content once more not to meet and argue as ere-while, but to meet and kiss; meet in a joint concurrence to save us, and set us free.

And indeed, *hoc opus*, 'there lies all'; how to set a song of these four parts in good harmony, how to make these meet at a love-day, how to satisfy Justice upon whom all the stay is.

And this, say I, no religion in the world doth or can do but the Christian. No choir sing this Psalm but ours, none make justice meet but it. Consequently, none quiet the conscience soundly but it; consequently, no religion but it. With all religions at odds they be, and so as they are fain to leave them so; for means in the world have they none how to make them meet. Not able for their lives to tender Justice a satisfaction, that will make her come in. The words next before are, 'that glory may dwell in our land'.[19] This glory doth dwell in our land indeed. And great cause have we all highly to bless God That hath made 'our lot to fall in so fair a ground'.[20] That we were not born to inherit a lie; that we were born to keep this feast of this meeting. For bid any of them all but shew you the way how to satisfy Justice soundly, and to make her come to this meeting; how God's word may be true, and His work just, and the sinner find mercy and be saved for all that – they cannot. The Christian only can do it, and none else. All beside for lack of this pass by the wounded man, and let him lie still and bleed to death.[21]

Bid the Turk. All he can say is, Mahomet's prayer shall be upon you. Mahomet's prayer, what is that? Say he were that he was not – a just man, a true prophet; what can his prayers do but move Mercy? But God's justice, how is that answered? Who shall satisfy that? Not prayers; – Justice is not moved with them, hears

---

[19] Psalm 85:9   [21] Luke 10:31-2
[20] Psalm 16:6

them not, goes on to sentence for all them. He can go no farther; he cannot make Justice meet.

Bid the Heathen. He says better yet than the Turk. They saw 'that without shedding of blood' there was no satisfying Justice, and so 'no remission of sin'.[22] To satisfy her, sacrifices they had of beasts. But 'it is impossible,' as the Apostle well notes, 'that the blood of bulls or goats should satisfy for our sins.'[23] A man sin, and a beast die! Justice will none of that. What then, will ye go as far as some did, 'the fruit of my body for the sin of my soul?'[24] Nor that neither. For if it were the first-born, the first-born was born in sin; and sin for sin can never satisfy. This meeting will not be there.

Bid the Jew. He can but tell you of his lamb neither. And while time was, that was not amiss; while it stood in reference to St John Baptist's Lamb, 'the Lamb of God' this day yeaned, as having the operation, the working, in the virtue of That. That being now past, there is no more in the Jews' than in the Gentiles' sacrifice. Beasts both; both short of satisfying. So for all that these can do or say, no meeting will there be had.

Only the Christian religion that shews the true way. There is One there thus speaketh to Justice; 'Sacrifice and sin-offerings Thou wouldst not have; then said I, Lo, I come.' He, 'of Whom it was written in the volume of the book that He should do that feat,' *corpus autem aptasti Mihi*, 'make Him a body to do it in', and He will do it.[25] Give Him an *ortus est*, let Him be but born, He will make them meet straight; – Justice and all. For all the world sees, if order could be taken that He, that the Son of God, the Word and Truth eternal would say, 'Lo, I come'; would take our nature upon Him, and in it 'lay down His soul an offering for sin';[26] there were good hope of contenting Justice, and that the meeting would go forward. *Deus sanguine in suo*, 'God with His blood'; – what sin in the world would not that serve for? What justice in Heaven or earth would not that satisfy? If ye speak of an expiation, a ransom, an ἀντάλλαγμα – Christ's own word – a perfect

---

[22] Hebrews 9:22
[23] Hebrews 10:4
[24] Micah 6:7

[25] Psalm 40:6ff.
[26] Ephesians 5:2; Isaiah 53:10

'commutation', there it is.[27] This had, Justice will meet, embrace, kiss Mercy, shake hands, join now friends; *Inveni enim in quo repropitier*, 'I have found that now, wherewith I hold myself fully content and pleased.'[28] This way ye shall make them meet, or else let it alone for ever.

Ver. 11. 'Truth shall bud out of the earth; and Righteousness shall look down from Heaven.'

And this is it the Christian religion sets before us; how the Son of the Most High God of Heaven and earth took on Him our nature, that in our nature, for our nature, He might make to God (even *stando in terminis justitiæ suæ*, as the schoolmen speak, 'standing on the terms of His most exact strict justice') a complete, full, every way sufficient satisfaction. And this, lo, makes the meeting. This honour hath the Christian religion above all other; this glory doth dwell in our land; that these four by Christ's birth in it are brought not only to *obviaverunt sibi*, but even to *et osculatæ sunt*.

And if this be the glory, be not they the shame of Christian profession that cherish in their bosoms, and entertain with stipends such as are come to this phrenzy I will call it, to say, what needs any satisfaction? What care we whether Justice·meet or no? that is in effect what needs Christ? Cannot God forgive offences to Him made, of His free goodness, of His mere mercy, without putting His Son to all this pain? Fond men! if He would quit His justice or waive His truth, He could; but His justice and truth are to Him as essential, as intrinsically essential, as His mercy; of equal regard, every way as dear to Him. Justice otherwise remains unsatisfied; and satisfied it must be either on Him or on us. For with beasts or prayers it will not be, and it will hold off till it be. If Justice be not so met with, it will meet with them; and they had better 'meet a she-bear robbed of her whelps',[29] than meet Justice out of Christ's presence.

To us they meet this day at the Child-house. For these great lights could not thus meet but they must portend some great matter, as it might be some great birth toward. The astrologers

---

[27] Matthew 16:26
[28] Job 33:24

[29] Proverbs 17:12

make us believe, that in the horoscope of Christ's Nativity there was a great trigon of I wot not what stars met together. Whether a trigon or no, this tetragon I am sure there was, these were all then in conjunction, all in the ascendant, all above the horizon at once at *orta est* 'the birth of' *veritas* 'the truth' *de terrâ* 'from the earth', the occasion of drawing these four together.

Veritas will fit Christ well Who of Himself said, *Ego sum Veritas*, 'I am the Truth.'[30] So is He – not that of the former verse which is but *veritas secunda*, the truth spoken or uttered forth; He the *Veritas prima*, 'the first Truth' within. That depends upon this. Then are the words uttered true, when there is an adequation between them and the mind. So, 'the first Truth' He is.

The first and last both. For now by His coming He is the adequation of the Word and the Work, the Promise and the Performance. That way He is Truth too, the truth of all types, the truth of all prophecies; for 'in Him are all the promises yea and Amen'[31] – yea, in the first truth; Amen, in the last. That actual verifying is the truth when all is done, and that He is by His birth.

And as the truth fits His nature, so doth earth man. Of whom God, 'earth thou art'; to whom the Prophet thrice over, 'Earth, hear the word of the Lord'; by whom the wise man, *Quid superbis?* 'Why should earth be proud?' *Germinet terra Salvatorem*, 'Let this earth bring forth a Saviour'[32] – be the *terra promissionis*, the blessed Virgin, who was in this the land of promise. So was this very place applied by Irenæus in his time, who touched the Apostles' times; so by Lactantius; so by St Hierom and St Augustine.[33] Those four meet in this sense, as do the four in the text. *Quid est veritas de terrâ orta? est Christus de fæminâ natus* [What is the truth born from the earth? It is Christ born of woman]. *Quid est Veritas? Filius Dei. Quid terra? Caro nostra.* 'What the truth? Christ. What the earth? our flesh.'[34] In those words they find this feast all.

---

[30] John 14:6
[31] 2 Corinthians 1:20
[32] Genesis 3:19; Jeremiah 22:29; Ecclesiasticus 10:9; Isaiah 45:8
[33] Irenæus, *Adversus Hæreses* (Against Heresies); Lactantius, *Divinæ Institutiones* (Divine Institutions); St Jerome, *Commentaria in Psalmos* (Commentary on the Psalms); St Augustine, *Enarrationes in Psalmos* (On Psalms)
[34] St Augustine, ibid.

For *orta est*, it is double; therefore *de terrâ* is well added. Another *ortus* he had *de Cœlo*; to wit, His heavenly Divine nature which as 'the day sprung from on high',[35] and He in regard of it called *oriens* by Zachary in the New Testament. But this here is *de terrâ*; for the word properly signifies 'the shooting forth of a sprig out of the ground', and He in regard of this *ortus* called 'the Branch' by Zachary in the Old.[36]

2. And there is more in *orta*. For, it is Rabbi Moses' note, that is properly when it springeth forth of itself, as the field flowers do, without any seed cast in by the hand of man; so, saith he, should the Messias come, take His nature not only in, but *de*, 'of' the earth. Not bring it with Him from Heaven, the error of the brain-sick Anabaptist, but take it of the earth; be 'the woman's seed', 'made of a woman',[37] 'out of the loins of David'; *Virga de radice Jesse*, 'the root of Jesse'[38] – nothing more plain.

3. And yet more from *orta est*. For that the truth, while it is yet unaccomplished but in promise only, it is but as the seed under ground, hid and covered with earth, as if no such thing were: as soon as ever it is actually accomplished as this day, then does it spring forth as it were, is to be seen above ground; then *orta est de terrâ*, in very deed.

Of the effect. Now births are and have been divers times the ending of great dissensions, as was this here. For by this birth took end the two great houses; an union of them by it.

First, by this Truth is gained; Truth will meet now. That truth will come to this Truth, *tanquam minus dignum ad magis dignum*, 'as the abstract to the archetype'. And Truth being now born of our nature, it will never we may be sure be against our nature; being come of the earth, it will be true to his own country; being made man, will be for man now all he can.

By this means one of the opposites is drawn away from the other; got to be on our side. It is three to one now. Righteousness is left all alone; and there is good hope she will not stand out long. For, lo, here is good news; first, that *respexit de Cœlo*, 'she yet looks down from Heaven now'.

---

[35] Luke 1:78
[36] Zechariah 3:8
[37] Galatians 4:4
[38] Isaiah 11:1

So as this birth in earth you see works in Heaven, and by name upon Righteousness there. For though there were none in Heaven but it wrought upon them, yet the Psalm mentions none but Righteousness. For of all, she the least likely; and if she be wrought on, the rest there is no doubt of. How can there? they are all won to us already.

With Righteousness it works two ways; first 'down she looks'. Whether it was that she missed Truth, to see what was become of her, and not finding her in Heaven cast her eye to the earth. But there, when she beheld *Verbum caro factum*, 'the Word flesh',[39] the truth freshly sprung there where it had been a strange plant long time before, *aspexit* and *respexit*, she looked and looked again at it. For a sight it was to move, to draw the eye; yea a sight for Heaven to be a spectator of, for the Angels to come down and look at, for Righteousness itself to do so too. Παρακύψαι is the Angels' word in St Peter;[40] διακύψαι is the Septuagint's word here. Both mean one thing. The Greek word is to 'look', as we say, 'wishly' at it, as if we would look διά, even 'through it'. The Hebrew word, – that is as if 'Righteousness did beat out a window', so desirous was she to behold this sight.

And no marvel; for what could Righteousness desire to see and satisfy herself with, that in Him was not to be seen? A clean birth, a holy life, an innocent death; a Spirit and a mouth without guile, a Soul and a body without sin. In Him she beheld them all. Them, and whatsoever else might yield her full satisfaction. 'Lay Judgment to the rule and Righteousness in the balance', nothing oblique will be found in Him, nothing but straight for the rule; nothing *minus habens*, but full weight for the balance.

Thus when 'Truth from the earth', then 'Righteousness from Heaven'. Then, but not before. Before Righteousness had no prospect, no window open this way. She turned away her face, shut her eyes, clapped to the casement, would not abide so much as to look hither – at us, a sort of forlorn sinners; – not vouchsafe us once the cast of her eye. The case is now altered. Upon this sight she is not only content in some sort to condescend to do it,

---

[39] John 1:14   [40] 1 Peter 1:12

but she breaks a window through to do it. And then, and ever since this *orta est*, she looks upon the earth with a good aspect; and a good aspect in these celestial lights is never without some good influence withal.

But then within a verse after, not only 'down she looks' but 'down she comes'.[41] Such a power attractive is there in this birth. And coming, she doth two things. 1. Meets first; for upon the view of this birth they all ran first and 'kissed the Son'. 2. And that done, Truth ran to Mercy and embraced her; and Righteousness to Peace, and 'kissed' her. They that had so long been parted, and stood out in difference, now meet and are made friends; howsoever before removed, *in ortu Veritatis obviaverunt sibi*; howsoever before estranged, now *osculatæ sunt*.

And at that birth of His well met they all, in Whom they meet all: the Truth He is, and *per viscera Misericordiæ* He came, 'through the tender mercies of our God', and He is made to us Righteousness, and He is our Peace.[42] All meet in Him, for indeed all He is; that no marvel they all four meet where He is That is all four.

And at this meeting Righteousness she was not so off-ward before but she is now as forward, as forward as any of the rest. Mark these three.

1. Lets not Peace prevent her, as Mercy did Truth; but as Mercy to Truth first, so she first to Peace – as forward as Mercy every way.

2. Nay more forward than Mercy, for Mercy doth but meet Truth, and there is all; but she as more affectionate not only 'meets Peace', but 'kisses her'. And indeed Righteousness was to do more, even to kiss, that it might be a pledge of forgetting all former unkindness, that we may be sure she is perfectly reconciled now.

3. And one more yet, to shew her the most forward of them all, out of the last verse.[43] At this meeting she follows not, draws not behind, she will not go with them; she is before, leaves them to come after and bear the train; she, as David, is before the Ark, puts St John Baptist from his office for the time; Righteousness is

---

[41] Psalm 85:13
[42] Luke 1:78; 1 Corinthians 1:30; Ephesians 2:14

[43] Psalm 85:13

his forerunner, 'Righteousness shall go before', tread the way before Him, the foremost now of all the company. By all which ye may know what a look it was she looked with from Heaven.

Thus ye see Christ by His coming 'hath pacified the things in Heaven'.[44] A peace of Hosannah is *pax in Cœlis*. There cannot be *pax in terris* till there it be first. But no sooner there it is, but it is peace in earth straight, which accordingly was this day proclaimed by the Angels. So by the virtue of this birth, Heaven is at peace with itself; and Heaven with earth is now at peace.[45] So is earth too with itself, and a fulfilling of the text by this meeting is there too.

The Jews, they represent Truth; to them it belongeth properly. For Truth was where were *eloquia Dei*, 'the oracles of God'; and they were with the Jews.[46] The Gentiles they claim by Mercy, that is their virtue. Where was Mercy but where was Misery? and where was Misery but with them that 'lay in darkness in the shadow of death?'[47] And that was the Gentiles' case before this *orta est*. But when 'the partition wall was broken down' and the two met in one, then also in a sense Mercy and Truth met together. So these two.

And so the other two likewise. For Righteousness she was where the Law was – for that the rule of Righteousness where the Covenant of the Old Testament was, 'Do this and live', the very voice of Justice. But Peace was where Christ was, in the Gospel. *Ipse est Pax nostra*, for 'He is our Peace'; Peace and Peace-maker both, *Qui fecit utrumque unum*, That hath made the Law and the Gospel, the Old Testament and the New, to be bound together now both in one volume.

Thus we have done with Christ. I would now apply this meeting to ourselves another while. For I ask, did this hold, did these meet only in Christ? Do they not in Christianity likewise? Yes, there too. With Christ came Christianity; look, what in His birth now, in the new birth of every one that shall be the better by it, even the same meeting of the very same virtues all.

Mercy and Truth first to meet. Truth of confession; confession

---

[44] Colossians 1:20
[45] Luke 2:14

[46] Romans 9:4, 3:2
[47] Luke 1:79

of our sins; which if with fig-leaves we seek to cover and confess not, 'there is no truth in us'.[48] And some truth there is to be, at least this truth, or no meeting with Mercy. But when this truth cometh forth, Mercy meeteth it straight. Will ye see the meeting? *Peccavi*, said David – there is Truth. *Transtulit Dominus peccatum*, saith Nathan[49] – there is Mercy; Mercy and Truth met together. *Homo in terris per Veritatem stimulatus peccâsse se confitebatur, et Deus in Cœlis per Misericordiam flexus confitentis miserebatur.* 'Truth pricked man to confess his sins; and Mercy moved God to pity him confessing,' and sends Mercy to meet Truth.[50]

Will ye go on to the other verse? It holds there too, this. For where a true confession is by man made, *Veritas de terrâ orta est*, 'Truth is budded out of the earth.' And so it must ere 'Righteousness will give us a good look from Heaven.' But will, as soon as it is: for when this truth springs freely from the earth to our own condemnation, immediately upon it, Righteousness shews herself from Heaven to our justification. Will ye see this too? 'Lord be merciful to me a sinner'[51] – there is truth from the earth. *Descendit domum suam justificatus,* – there is Righteousness from Heaven.

But will ye mark, here are two truths, and in either verse one. This latter is the truth of *veritas orta est*, of Christ's religion. And in this treaty it was an article of *Imprimis*, Mercy not to meet any but them that profess the truth of Christ's birth from the earth. Both these were born together; by and by upon the birth of Christ the truth, the other birth also of Christian truth, did flourish and spread itself all over the earth. The whole world before given over, and even grown over with idolatry, quite covered with the mist of error and ignorance, began then to entertain the Christian profession, and by it to 'worship God in spirit and truth' – the true religion which is never true, if it have not this meeting. And this meeting it cannot have, if it have not the means of it, *ortus Veritatis de terrâ*.

The same say we likewise for the 'Righteousness which looked down' and shewed herself. It was not that of the Law which

---

[48] 1 John 1:8
[49] 2 Samuel 12:13
[50] Hugo of St Victor, op. cit.
[51] Luke 18:14

never came past the top of Mount Sinai, but a new Righteousness cast in a new mould; a Heavenly one which never saw the earth nor the earth it before, before this birth – which is the righteousness of Christ revealed in His Gospel; when that truth sprang, this righteousness looked down upon it.

Now as this of Mercy and Truth enter us; so Truth – not Truth alone, but Truth with Truth's pair – with Righteousness, carry us forward to God. Truth is not enough; not the truth of religion never so known, never so professed; not without Righteousness. Truth is but the light to guide us, Righteousness is the way to bring us thither. A light is to see by; a way is to go in; so is Righteousness. It follows straight, *ponet gressus in viâ*, 'Righteousness shall set us in the way' of His steps.[52] Steps, that is the course of life. For *scienti*, by knowledge of the truth and not *facienti* by the practice of righteousness, *peccatum est illi* [to him it is sin], saith St James; and *plagæ multæ* [many stripes], saith St James' Master.[53] Sin in that man that serves these two is less pardonable, and more punishable than in any other.

And then, turn Righteousness to Peace, and they will not meet barely but more than meet, 'kiss' in sign there is between them more than ordinary affection. *Fac Justitiam et habebis Pacem* [Do good and seek peace]; St Augustine stands much on this. 'Eschew evil and do good,' saith he – there is Righteousness.[54] And then, 'seek Peace,' and ye shall not be long in seeking it; she will come forth herself to meet Righteousness and kiss her. And this he assures us as a certain sign to know on the one side true Righteousness, for that tends to Peace not to questions and brabbles whereof there never will be end; so on the other side true Peace that kisses Righteousness comes not together like Samson's foxes by the tails,[55] by indirect means, but clearly and fairly; such means as all the world will confess to be right and good.

Now mark the order how they stand. Mercy leads to Truth, and the knowledge of it; and Truth to Righteousness, and the practice of it; and Righteousness to Peace, and the ways of it –

---

[52] Psalm 85:13
[53] James 4:17; Luke 12:47

[54] Psalm 34:14; St Augustine, op. cit.
[55] Judges 15:4

'guides our feet' first 'into the way of Peace'.[56] And such a way shall there always be, do all the controversy-writers what they can, a fair way agreed upon of all sides, questioned by none, in which whoso orders his steps aright 'may see the salvation of our God'. Even the way here chalked out before us; to shew Mercy, and speak Truth; do Righteousness, and follow Peace. And by this rule proceeding in the points whereto we are come already, even those truths wherein we are otherwise minded would in due time be revealed unto us.

This is Zachary's peace; and this of his well followed in the end will bring us Simeon's peace, *nunc dimittis in pace*; to be dismissed, 'to depart hence in peace'.[57] And *pax in novissimo*, 'peace at the latter end', is worth all. Peace in the end is a blessed end, and the beginning of a peace which never shall have end. Mercy our beginning, and Peace our end. This for the meeting; as in Christ, so in Christianity or the course of a Christian man's life.

Now a word for the continuance of this meeting. For I ask again, met they to part? By no means; but as they be together now, so to continue still. We had much ado to get them together thus. Now we have them so, let us keep them so in any wise. For as this meeting made Christianity first; so there is nothing mars it but the breaking it off again; no greater bane to it than the parting of these.

Let me tell you this: St Augustine is very earnest upon this point of the keeping of Righteousness and Peace upon this Psalm and this verse, and of Truth and Mercy together in the next, upon *Misericors* and *Verax* against them that would lay hold on Mercy and let go Truth. O, saith he, that will not be; they met together, they will not part now; either without either will not be had. And so of the two others. There be that would have Peace, and pass by Righteousness. *Tu forte unam habere vis, et alteram non vis*, saith he, 'you would gladly have one – Peace; and for Righteousness you could be contented to spare it. Ask any, would you have Peace? With all my heart, he will answer. There is no having one without the other; *osculantur hæ, amant hæ*, why they kiss, they love

[56] Luke 1:79   [57] Luke 2:29

together.' *Si amicam Pacis non amaveris, non amabit te Pax*, 'if ye love not her friend, that is Righteousness, she will none of your love.' Take that from St Augustine.

Set this down then; Christianity is a meeting. One cannot meet. Two there must be, and they may. But it is not a meeting of two, but of two with two; so, no less than four. As Christ Himself was not one nature, so neither doth Christianity consist in any one virtue; not under four. There is a *quaternion* in Christ; His 1. Essence and His 2. Person, Οὐσία and *Hypostasis, in Divinis.* His 3. Flesh and His 4. reasonable Soul, *in humanis.* Answerable to these four are these here, these four to His four.

And as it is a meeting, so a cross meeting of four virtues that seem to be in a kind of opposition, as hath been noted. No matter for that. They will make the better refraction; the cool of one allay the heat, the moist of one temper the drought of the other. The soft virtues need to be quickened, the more forward to be kept from *altum sapere* [going too far]. So are the elements of which our body, so are the four winds of which our breath doth consist which gives us life. And these in the text have an analogy or correspondence with the elements, observed by the ancients. 1. Truth as the 'earth, which is not moved at any time.'[58] 2. *Quasi fluvius pax*, saith Esay, 'peace as a water-stream', 'the quills whereof make glad the City of our God.'[59] 3. Mercy we breathe and live by, no less than we do by air; and 4. Righteousness, she *ventura est judicare sæculum per ignem* [has come to judge the age with fire], in that element.[60]

You may happen to find one of these in Scripture stood much upon, and of the other three nothing said there, but all left out. Conceive of it as a figure, Synecdoche they call it. As ye have here man called earth; yet is he not earth alone, but all the other three elements as well. No more is Christianity any one but by Synecdoche, but in very deed a meeting of them all four.

It deceived the Gnostic, this place; 'This is eternal life to know thee.'[61] Knowledge, saith he, is it, as if it were all; and so he bade

---

[58] Psalm 93:1
[59] Isaiah 66:12; Psalm 46:4 ('quills', streams)
[60] Isaiah 66:16
[61] John 17:3

care for nothing else but to know, and knowing live as they list. The Encratite, he was as far gone the other way; he lived straightly, and his tenet was, *Non est curandum quid quisque credat, id curandum modo quod quisque faciat*, 'So that ye hold a straight course of life, it skills not what ye hold in point of faith.'[62] No meeting with these, single virtues all.

Yes, it skills. For both these were wrong, both go for heretics. Christianity is a meeting, and to this meeting there go *pia dogmata* as well as *bona opera* – Righteousness as well as Truth. Err not this error then, to single any out as it were in disgrace of the rest; say not one will serve the turn, – what should we do with the rest of the four. Take not a figure, and make of it a plain speech; seek not to be saved by Synecdoche. Each of these is a quarter of Christianity, you shall never while you live make it serve for the whole.

The truth is, – sever them, and farewell all. Take any one from the rest, and it is as much as the whole is worth. For, as Bernard well observed, *non sunt virtutes si separentur*, 'upon their separation they cease to be virtues.'[63] For how loose a thing is mercy, if it be quite devoid of justice? We call it foolish pity. And how harsh a thing justice, if it be utterly without all temper of mercy! *Summa injuria* then, that is 'injustice at the highest'. Mercy, take Truth away, what hold is there of it? Who will trust it? Truth, take Mercy from it, it is severity rather than verity. Then Righteousness without Peace, certainly wrong is much better – better than perpetual brabbling. And Peace without Righteousness, better a sword far. This, if you sunder them. But temper these together, and how blessed a mixture! Set a song of all four, and how heavenly a melody!

Entertain them then all four: 1. hope in Mercy; 2. faith in Truth; 3. fear of Righteousness; 4. love of Peace; *O quam præclara concordia!* O how loving a knot! how by all means to be maintained! how great pity to part it!

A little of the time now, when this meeting would be. No time amiss, no day in the year but upon entreaty they will be got to meet. Yet if any one day have a prerogative more than another, of

---

[62] Irenaues, *Adversos Hæreses* (Against Heresies [including Gnosticism]); Epithanius of Constantia, *Adversos Hæreses*, II.i, *Adversos Encratites* (Against the Encratites)
[63] St Bernard, op. cit.

all the days in the year on this day most kindly; the day we hold holy to the memory of this meeting; the day of *orta est*, the occasion of it. In remembrance of the first meeting then, they are apt and willing to meet upon it again; forward ever to meet the day they first met of themselves. But Christ this day born, this day to meet of course. One special end that He was born was that at His birth this meeting might be. If today then they should not meet, that were in a sort to evacuate Christ's birth, if there should be a *Veritas orta* without an *obviaverunt sibi*; so that if we procure it not, we had as good keep no feast at all.

What is then the proper work of this day, but still to renew this meeting on it? For Christ's birth we cannot entertain, but all these we must too, necessary attendants upon it every one. They be the virtues of His Nativity, these. At His birth Christ bethought Himself of all the virtues which He would have to attend on Him then; and these He made choice of then, and for ever, to be the virtues of this feast.

The sooner and the better to procure this meeting, the Church meets us, as Melchizedek did Abraham, 'with bread and wine', but of a higher nature than his far; prepares ever this day a lovefeast, whereat they may the rather meet. Where Truth from the earth may look up to Heaven and confess, and Righteousness from Heaven may look down to earth and pardon; where we may shew Mercy in giving where need is; and offer Peace in forgiving where cause is; that so there may be an *obviaverunt*, a 'meeting' of all hands.

And even so then let there be. So may our end be as the end of the first verse, in peace; and as the end of the second, in Heaven! So may all the blessings that came to mankind by this meeting, or by the birth of Christ the cause of it, meet in us and remain upon us, till as we now meet together at the birth, so we may then meet in a 'perfect man in the measure of the fulness of the age of Christ';[64] as meet now at the Lamb's yeaning, so meet then at the Lamb's marriage; 'be caught up in the clouds then to meet Him',[65] and there to reign for ever with Him in His Kingdom of Glory!

---

[63] Ephesians 4:13   [64] 1 Thessalonians 4:17

A Sermon

PREACHED BEFORE

THE KING'S MAJESTY, AT HOLYROOD-HOUSE

on the Eighth of June, A.D. MDCXVII, Being Whit-Sunday.

Luke iv: 18, 19.

> *The Spirit of the Lord is upon Me, because He hath anointed Me, that I should preach the Gospel to the poor; He hath sent Me, that I should heal the broken-hearted, that I should preach deliverance to the captives, and recovering of sight to the blind, and that I should set at liberty them that are bruised,*
>
> *And that I should preach the acceptable year of the Lord.*
>
> [*Spiritus Domini super Me, propter quod unxit Me; evangelizare pauperibus misit Me, sanare contritos corde,*
>
> *Prædicare captivis remissionem, et cæcis visum, dimittere confractos in remissionem, prædicare annum Domini acceptum, et diem retributionis.* Latin Vulg.]
>
> [*The Spirit of the Lord is upon Me, because He hath anointed Me to preach the Gospel to the poor; He hath sent Me to heal the broken-hearted, to preach deliverance to the captives, and recovering of sight to the blind, to set at liberty them that are bruised.*
>
> *To preach the acceptable year of the Lord.* Authorized Version]

We are fallen here upon Christ's first sermon, preached at Nazareth; and upon His very text. This I have read you was His text, taken out of the Prophet Esay, the sixty-first chapter, and first verse. There was no fear Christ would have ranged far from His matter, if He had taken none; yet He took a text, to teach us thereby to do the like. To keep us within; not to fly out, or preach much, either without, or besides the book.

And He took His text for the day, as is plain by His application, 'This day is this Scripture fulfilled in your ears.'[1] 'This day this

---

[1] Luke 4:21

45

Scripture.' Our Master's Scripture was for the day; so would ours be.

For the day; and for the present occasion. For among the writers it is generally received, that when our Saviour made this sermon, that year it was with the Jews the year of jubilee. And that therefore He told them, it was fulfilled in their ears, they might hear the trumpets sound to it. If it were so, this text of 'the acceptable year' was as apposite as could be chosen. That, it seems, He turned the book purposely to find it; out of it to speak to them of the true jubilee.

And if it were so, the year of jubilee, it was the last that ever they held. For before fifty years came about again, they were swept away – Temple, sacrifice, jubilee, people and all. The jubilees of the Law then failing, being come to their period, comes Christ with His; with a new jubilee of the Gospel, the true one, as whereof those of theirs were but shadows only, which jubilee of the Gospel was 'the acceptable year' which Esay here meant.

Will ye then give me leave now to say of this text of our Saviour's, This Scripture suits well with this day, is fulfilled in it three ways? In the 1. coming of the Spirit; 2. the end for which, to send to proclaim; 3. the matter which, to proclaim a jubilee; 4. and a fourth I will add, of a present occasion, as fit every way.

First, it is the coming of the Spirit. And this day the Spirit came. And the coming of the Spirit, in the text here upon Christ, was the cause of the coming of the Spirit, this day, upon the Apostles. From this coming upon Him, came the coming upon them; *super Petrum, super Jacobum, super* all the rest; upon them, and upon us all, from this *super Me.* All our anointings are but drops from His anointing; all our missions and commissions, but quills, as we say, out of this commission here, *misit Me. Sicut misit Me, Ego mitto vos.* He sent Me, 'as He sent Me, I send you.'[2] By that, and by no other commission, did they, or do we, or shall ever any come.

That first, and this second; the *misit* and the *ad.* Why came the

2 John 20:21

46

Spirit on Christ? To send Him. Send Him to what? *ad evangelizandum*. And why came the Spirit on the Twelve this day, but for the very same end? And it came therefore for the purpose, in the shape of tongues. It is the office of the tongue to be a trumpet, to proclaim. It serves for no other end.

To proclaim what? 'the acceptable year of the Lord', that is, the Jubilee. Now fifty is the number of the jubilee; which number agreeth well with this feast, this feast of Pentecost. What the one in years, the other in days. So that this is the jubilee, as it were, of the year, or the yearly memory of the year of jubilee. That, the Pentecost of years; this, the jubilee of days. These three for the day.

And may we not add a fourth from the present occasion? I take it we may; and that not unfit neither, as peculiar to this very year, rather than to any other. There falleth out, lightly, but one jubilee in a man's age. 1. And this present year is yet the jubilee year of your Majesty's life and reign. 2. And this day is the jubilee day of that year. 3. And yet further, if we take not jubilee for the time, but for the joy – for the word jubilee is taken, as for the time of the joy, so for the joy of the time – and so refer it to the late great joy and jubilee, at your majesty's receiving hither to your Nazareth, the country where you were brought up, which then was fulfilled in your ears; our ears, I am sure, were filled full with it. So that, first and last, the text suits with the day, and both suit well with the present occasion.

To return to our Saviour, Who standing now with His loins girt, ready to go about the errand He came for, as the manner is, He was first to read His commission. This it is, the words I have read, drawn and ready penned for Him long before by the Prophet Esay here, who had the honour to be the registrar of this, and divers other instruments, touching Christ's natures, Person, and offices. And, upon the reading of this, He entered in His office.

You may plainly know, it was His inauguration, this, or first entering on His office, by the proclamation following, of opening the gaol, and letting the prisoners go free. So is ever the fashion of princes, to make the joy general, of their coming to their kingdoms: to release those that stand committed; to grant free and general pardons to all that will sue for them; to be at the charge of *missilia*, certain new pieces of coin, to be cast abroad among the people.

Accordingly, were there this day of the Spirit's coming, by one sermon of St Peter's, three thousand set at liberty that had been captives before under Satan. A largess of new tongues, as it were *missilia*, cast down from Heaven. A general pardon proclaimed, even for them that had been 'the betrayers and murderers'[3] of the Son of God, if they would come in. That it was, indeed, a right day of jubilee. And this is the sum of all.

I. The parts as they lie, are these: 1. First, of the Spirit's being on Christ; 2. Anointing Him; 3. Sending Him. These three.

II. Then, whereto He was so anointed and sent; to preach the Gospel, or glad tidings (glad tidings, or Gospel, both are one) and that even to the poor.

III. Thirdly, whereof the tidings is; of an excellent physician, a physician of the heart, one that can cure a broken heart.

IV. Of these hearts. 1. How they came broken first, and there are three ways here set down. 1. By being captives; 2. by being in a dark dungeon, where their sight was even taken from them; 3. By being there in irons so as they were even bruised with them. Three, able, I think, to break any man's heart alive.

2. Then, how came they cured. And that is by good news. Two proclamations, for κηρύξαι 'to proclaim' is twice repeated: 1. One, containing a particular remedy of those three several maladies; 1. Of a party, one with a ransom, or redemption for the captives; 2. with an engine, or tool, to knock off their irons; 3. with the keys of the prison, to let them out. And this to begin with. 2. Then, to conclude, with a second proclamation, that makes up all – of a year of jubilee; and so of restitution of them to their former forfeited estates, by God's accepting them to favour, this acceptable time.

This is the sum of Christ's commission here read; and indeed, a brief of His offices, all three. 1. In preaching the glad news of the Gospel – of His prophecy; 2. In granting pardon, and enlarging prisoners – of His kingdom. 3. In proclaiming a jubilee – of His

---

[3] Acts 7:52

Priesthood, for that the peculiar of the Priest's office. So all are in, that pertain to Christ. And all, that to Jesus too, Who sheweth Himself Jesus in nothing so much, as in being the physician of a broken contrite heart.

We cannot better begin, than with the Blessed Trinity. In the three first words, the three Persons reasonable clear. 1. The Spirit: 2. He, Whose the Spirit – *Domini*; 3. He, on Whom the Spirit, *super Me*.

'The Spirit', that is, the Holy Ghost. He Whose the Spirit, God the Father. He on Whom the Spirit, our Saviour Christ. He, the *super Quem* here.

These three distinct: 1. the Spirit, from the 2. Lord, Whose the Spirit is; 1. the Spirit That was upon, 3. from Him It was upon. Yet all three in one joint concurrence to one and the same work, the jubilee of the Gospel.

'Upon Me', is Christ's person. But His Person only, according to one of His natures, His human. The Spirit was not upon Him, but as He was man. These three; 1. to be sent, 2. to be anointed, 3. to have a *super Eum*, savour of inferiority, all, to the Sender, Anointer, Superior. And so indeed for us, He became lower than in Himself He was. 'In the similitude of sinful flesh,'[4] had a Spirit to anoint Him; *in formâ servi* [in the form of a servant],[5] had a Lord to send Him about the message here.

But, that Christ suffer not in His honour, we supply; that the Spirit Who is here said to be *Spiritus Domini*, is elsewhere said to be *Spiritus Christi* – 'the Spirit of the Father', and 'the Spirit of the Son', both. The Spirit That sent Him here, sent by Him elsewhere, 'Whom I will send'.[6] This sets Him upright again. As the one shews Him to be Man, so the other, to be God. And as God He hath no superior; no Lord to own Him, no Spirit to anoint Him.

And, if I mistake not, a kind of inkling of thus much is even in the very words. The word 'Lord' in Esay, is plural; and so more Persons than one, Whose the Spirit is, and from Whom He proceeds. And if you would know how many, in Esay the words be

---

[4] Romans 8:3
[5] Philippians 2:7

[6] Romans 8:9; Matthew 10:20; Galatians 4:6; John 15:26

two: so, not a single proceeding from one, but a double from two, as the word is double. St Basil saith it short, 'Ὡς Θεὸς χορηγεῖ, ὡς ἄνθρωπος δέχεται, 'As God He sends it, as man He receives it.' Upon Him, as man; from Him, as God.

Of Him then, as man, three things here are said: 'the Spirit' 1. was 'upon' Him; 2. 'anointed' Him; 3. 'sent' Him. But it is said, 'The Spirit is upon Me, because He hath anointed Me;' so as the anointing is set, as the ἕνεκεν οὖ, or cause, why He was upon Him. And then that, His anointing, as the cause, is first in nature. But it cannot be conceived but the Spirit must be also upon Him, to anoint Him; the Spirit is the *Unction*: the Spirit then was upon Him, two several times, for two several ends. 1. To anoint Him; 2. and after He was anointed, to send Him; the second. Of this anointing we are to touch, 1. when it was; 2. with what it was; 3. and how it comes to be termed anointing.

When was He thus 'anointed'? Not now, or here, first, but long before; even from the very time of His conceiving. When 'the Word became flesh',[7] the flesh with the Word, and by means of it with the whole Deity, was 'anointed' all over, and by virtue thereof filled with the fulness of all grace. For this we are to hold; that Christ was ever Christ, that is, ever 'anointed', from the very first instant of all; He was never un-anointed, not one moment.

'Anointed' with what? I have already told you, with the Deity, by virtue of the Personal union of the second Person of the Deity. Why then is the Holy Ghost called the Unction? Why is Christ expressly said to be anointed with the Holy Ghost? why not with the Father as well?

Why not? to retain to each Person His own peculiar, His proper act, in this common work of them all; or, as the Hebrews speak, to keep every word upon his right wheel.

Father, is a term of nature. So to the Father we ascribe what the Son hath by nature. For that He is the Son, is of nature, not of grace.

But that the manhood is taken into God, that was not of nature, but of grace. And what is of grace, is ever properly ascribed to

---

[7] John 1:14

50

the Spirit. 'There are diversities of graces', all from the 'same Spirit'.[8] And the proceeding of grace from it, not as by nature, but *ubi vult*, 'blows where it lists' freely.[9] All then, of grace, proceeding from the Spirit: accordingly, the conception of Christ's flesh, and the sending it with the fulness of grace, or anointing it, is ascribed to the Spirit.

But this enduing with grace, how comes it to be called anointing? for nothing, but for the resemblance it hath with an ointment. An ointment is a composition we know; the ingredients of it, oil and sweet odours. By virtue of the oil it soaks even into the bones, saith the Psalm;[10] but it works upon the joints and sinews sensibly, makes them supple and lithe, and so the more fresh and active to bestir themselves. By virtue of the sweet odours mixed with it, it works upon the spirits and senses; cheers him and makes him 'glad', that is anointed with it.[11] And not him alone, but all that are about and near him, *qui in odore unguentorum*,[12] that take delight in his company, to go and to run with him, and all for the fragrant sweet scent they feel to come from him.

Of which two, the oil represents the virtue of the power of the Spirit, piercing through, but gently, like oil. The odours, the sweet comfort of the graces that proceed from the Holy Ghost. Nothing more like. And this for His anointing.

Now the same Spirit That was thus upon Him at His conception to anoint Him, was even now upon Him again, to manifest, and to send Him. When? at His baptism, a little before. Not secretly, as then at His conception, but in a visible shape upon Him, before a great concourse of people, (to shew there ought to be an outward calling) what time the dove laid that, which in it is answerable to our hands, upon Him.[13]

Not, to endue Him with aught – that was done before long – but to manifest to all, this was He; this, the party before anointed, and now sent, that they might take heed to Him. It was the Holy Ghost's first Epiphany this, He was never seen before; but Christ's

[8] 1 Corinthians 12:4
[9] John 3:8
[10] Psalm 109:18
[11] Psalm 45:8
[12] Song of Solomon 1:3
[13] Luke 3:22

second Epiphany. The other at His birth, or coming into the world; this now at His calling, or sending into the world. That first, to enable Him to His office; this, to design Him to it. By that, furnished for it; by this, sent, severed, and set about the work He came for.

But before we come to the work, let us first reflect a little upon these; they serve our turn, are for our direction. These both were done to Christ, to the end He might teach the Church, that the same were to be on them who in Christ's stead are employed in the same business, *ad evangelizandum*. The Holy Ghost, to be upon them; upon them, to anoint them, and to send them, both; but first to anoint, then to send them. To be, and in this order to be. Unless they be first 'anointed', not to be sent; and though never so 'anointed', not to start out of themselves, but to stay till they be sent.

The Spirit to be upon them; the same That upon Christ, though not in the same, but in a broad and a large difference, or degree, of being. Upon Him without measure; not so, on us; but on some less – the measure of the hin; on some more – the measure of the ephah; but every one, his homer at least. Some feathers of the dove, as it were, though not the dove itself; not the whole Spirit entire, as upon Him.

On His head the whole box of ointment was broken, which from Him ran down upon the Apostles, somewhat more fresh and full; and ever, the further, the thinner, as the nature of things liquid is; but some small streams trickle down even to us, and to our times still.

This on-being shews itself first, in that which stands first – the anointing.

I shall not need tell you, the Spirit comes not upon us now at our conception in the womb, to anoint us there. No; we behove to light our lamps oft, and to spend much oil at our studies, ere we can attain it. This way come we to our anointing now, by books; this book chiefly, but in a good part also, by the books of the ancient Fathers and lights of the Church, in whom the scent of this ointment was fresh, and the temper true; on whose writings it lieth thick, and we thence strike it off, and gather it safely.

You will mark, the anointing is set for the cause; 'The Spirit is is upon Me, because He hath anointed Me.' Then *sublatâ causâ*, and, *a sensu contrario* [by reversing the argument, and, in the opposite sense], the Spirit is not upon Me, because He hath not anointed Me. Again, 'because He hath anointed Me, He hath sent Me.' And then it follows, because He hath not anointed Me, He hath not sent Me. No speaking of the Spirit's on-being; no talk of sent by Him, without it. Where be they then that say, The less anointing, the more of the Spirit? Indeed, the more blind, the more bold; and so the fitter to go on some other errand perhaps, but not this.

No, no; the Spirit makes none of these dry missions, sends none of these same *inuncti* [unanointed], such as have never a feather of the Dove's wing, nor any spark of the fire of this day, not so much as a drop of this ointment. You shall smell them straight that have it; 'the myrrh, aloes, and cassia will make you glad.'[14] And you shall even as soon find the others. Either they want odour: – anointed I cannot say, but besmeared with some unctuous stuff (go to, be it oil) that gives a glibness to the tongue to talk much and long, but no more scent in it than in a dry stick; no odours in it at all. Either odours they want, I say, or their odours are not laid in oil. For if in oil, you shall not smell them so for a few set sermons; if they be anointed, not perfumed or washed, for such Divines we have. If it be but some sweet water, out of a casting-bottle, the scent will away soon; water-colours, or water-odours, will not last. But if laid in oil throughly, they will; fear them not. To them that are stuffed, I know all is one; they that have their senses about them, will soon put a difference.

But what? If he be 'anointed', then turn him off hardly with no more ado, without stay for any sending at all? Nay, we see here, only anointing served not Christ Himself. He was 'sent', and outwardly 'sent' besides. Messias He was, in regard of His anointing; Shiloh He was too, in regard of His sending. If you love your eyes, wash them in the water of Shiloh, that is by interpretation 'sent'.[15] Or, to speak in the style of the text, as He was Christ for His anointing, so was He an Apostle for His sending. So is He

---

[14] Psalm 45:8   [15] John 9:7

53

called 'the Apostle of our profession',[16] with plain reference to ἀπέσταλκε here, the word in the text.

Unction then is to go before, but not to go alone, mission is to follow; and no man, though never so *perunctus, eo ipso* [anointed by Himself] to stir, *nisi qui vocatus erit sicut Aaron*, 'unless he be called, as was Aaron';[17] unless he be sent, as Christ here was; for fear of *currebant et non mittebam eos* [I have not sent these prophets, yet they ran], in the Prophet;[18] or of 'How shall they preach unless they be sent?' in the Apostle.[19] For his life he knew not, if neither Aaron nor Christ, how any might step up without calling, sending, ordaining, laying on of hands: all are one.

And mark well this, that the Holy Ghost came upon Christ alike for both, that there is the Holy Ghost no less in this sending than in the anointing. The very calling itself is a 'grace', expressly so called, Romans the twelfth, and Ephesians the third, and in divers places else.[20] Every grace is of the Holy Ghost; and goeth ever, and is termed by the name of the Holy Ghost usually. And in this sense the Holy Ghost is given and received in Holy Orders, and we do well avow that we say, 'Receive the Holy Ghost.'

But we have not all, when we have both these; for shall we so dwell upon anointing and sending, as we pass by the *super Me*, the first of all the three, and sure not the last to be looked after? A plain note it is but not without use, this situation of the Spirit, that He is *super*. For if He be *super*, we be *sub*. That we be careful then to preserve Him in His *super*, to keep Him in His due place, that is, 'above'. In sign whereof the dove hovered aloft over Christ, and 'came down upon Him'; and in sign thereof we submit our heads in anointing to have the oil poured upon, we submit our heads in ordaining to have hands laid upon them. So submit we do, in sign that submit we must; that not only mission, but submission is a sign of one truly called to this business. Somewhat of the dove there must be, needs; meekness, humbleness of mind.

But lightly you shall find it, that those that be *neque uncti neque*

---

[16] Hebrews 3:1
[17] Hebrews 5:4
[18] Jeremiah 23:21
[19] Romans 10:15
[20] Romans 12:3; Ephesians 3:7

loti, 'neither anointed nor scarce well washed'; the less ointment, the worse sending, the farther from this submissive, humble, mind. That above? Nay, any above? Nay, they inferior to none. That above, and they under? Nay under no Spirit; no *super*, they. Of all prepositions they endure not that, not *super*; all equal, all even at least. Their spirit not subject to the spirit of the Prophets, nor of the Apostles neither, if they were now alive; but bear themselves so high, do *tam altum spirare* [aspire so high], as if this Spirit were their underling, and their ghost above the Holy Ghost. There may be a sprite in them, there is no Spirit upon them that endure no *super*, none above them. So now we have all we should; unction out of *unxit*, mission out of *misit*, submission out of *super Me*.

Forward now. 'Upon Me.' How know we that? 'Because He hath anointed Me.' 'Anointed', to what end? 'To send.' 'Send' whereto? That follows now. Both whereto and whom to. 1. Whereto? 'To bring good tidings.' 2. Whom to? 'To the poor'.

1. Whereto? If the Spirit send Christ, He will send Him with the best sending; and the best sending is to be sent with a message of good news; the best, and the best welcome. We all strive to bear them, we all love to have them brought; the Gospel is nothing else but a message of good tidings. And Christ, as in regard of His sending, an Apostle, the Arch-Apostle, so in regard of that He is sent with, an Evangelist, the Arch-Evangelist. Christ is to anoint: this is a kind of anointing; and no ointment so precious, no oil so supple, no odour so pleasing, as the knowledge of it; called therefore by the Apostle *odor vitæ*, 'the savour of life unto life', in them that receive it.

2. Send with this, and to whom? 'To the poor.' You may know it is the Spirit of God by this. That Spirit it is; and they that 'anointed' with It, take care of the poor. The spirit of the world, and they that anointed with it take little keep to evangelize any such, any poor souls. But in the tidings of the Gospel they are not left out; taken in by name, we see: in sending those tidings there is none excluded. 'No respect of persons with God.'[21] None of

---

[21] Acts 10:34

nations; to every nation, Gentile and Jew: none of conditions; to every condition, poor and rich. To them that of all other are the least likely. They are not troubled with much worldly good news; seldom come there any posts to them with such. But the good news of the Gospel reacheth even to the meanest. And reaching to them it must needs be general, this news. If to them that of all other least likely, then certainly to all. *Etiam pauperibus* is, as if He had said, even to poor and all, by way of extent, *ampliando*. But no ways to engross it, or appropriate it to them only. The tidings of the Gospel are as well for 'Lydia the purple seller' as for 'Simon the tanner'; for 'the Areopagite', the judge at Athens, as for 'the jailor' at Philippi; for 'the elect lady' as for widow 'Dorcas'; for the 'Lord Treasurer of Ethiopia' as for 'the beggar at the beautiful gate of the temple'; for 'the household of Cæsar' as for 'the household of Stephanas'; yea and, if he will, for 'king Agrippa' too.[22]

But if you will have *pauperibus* a restringent, you may; but then you must take it for 'poor in spirit',[23] with whom our Saviour begins His beatitudes in the mount; – the poverty to be found in all. As indeed I know none so rich but needs these tidings; all to feel the want of them in their spirits; no *Dicis quia dives sum* [Because thou sayest, I am rich];[24] as few sparks of a Pharisee as may be, in them that will be interested in it.

Well, we see to whom: what may these news be? News of a new physician, Καρδίατρος, *Medicus cordis*, one that can give physic to heal a broken heart. And news of such an one is good news indeed. They that can cure parts less principal, broken arms or legs, or limbs out of joint, are much made of, and sent for far and near. What say you to one that is good at a broken heart? make that whole, set that in joint again, if it happen to be out? So they understood it plainly by their speech to Him after, *Medice cura Teipsum* [Physician heal thyself].[25]

The heart, sure, is the part all other we would most gladly have well. 'Give me any grief to the grief of the heart,' saith one

---

[22] Acts 16:14; Acts 10:6; Acts 17:34; Acts 16:30; 2 John 1; Acts 9:36; Acts 8:27; Acts 3:2; Philippians 4:22; 1 Corinthians 1:16; Acts 26:27

[23] Matthew 5:3   [25] Luke 4:23

[24] Revelation 3:17

that knew what he said.[26] *Omni custodia custodi cor*, saith Solomon, 'keep thy heart above all':[27] if that be down, all is down; look to that in any wise. Now it is most proper for the Spirit to deal with that part; it is the fountain of the spirits of life, and whither indeed none can come but the Spirit, to do any cure to purpose; that if Christ, if the Spirit take it not in hand, all cures else are but palliative; they may drive it away for a while, it will come again worse than ever. Now then to *Medice cura*, as Christ after saith, to this new cure.

In every cure, our rule is first to look to *de causis morborum*, how the heart can be broken; then after, *de methodo medendi*, the way here to help it.

How comes the heart broken? The common hammer that breaks them is some bodily or worldly cross, such as we commonly call heart-breakings. There be here in the text three strokes of this hammer, able I think to break any heart in the world.

1. Captivity. They be captives first; and captives and caitiffs, in our speech, sound much upon one. It is sure a condition able to make any man 'hang up his harp', and 'sit weeping by the waters of Babylon'.[28] There is one stroke.

2. There follows another, worse yet. For in Babylon, though they were captives, yet went they abroad, had their liberty. These here are in prison; and in some blind hole there, as it might be in the dungeon, where they see nothing. That, I take it, is meant by blind here in the text; blind for want of light, not for want of sight, though those two both come to one, are convertible. They that be blind, say they are dark; and they that be in the dark, for the time are deprived of sight, have no manner use of it at all, no more than a blind man. Now they that row in the galleys yet this comfort they have, they see the light; and if a man see nothing else, the light of itself is comfortable.[29] And a great stroke of the hammer it is, not to have so much as that poor comfort left them.

3. But yet are not we at the worst; one stroke more. For one may be in the dungeon and yet have his limbs at large, his hands

---

[26] Ecclesiasticus 25:13
[27] Proverbs 4:23

[28] Psalm 137:1-2
[29] Ecclesiastes 11:7

and feet at liberty. But so have not those in the text, but are in irons; and those so heavy and so pinching, as they are even τεθραυσμένοι, 'bruised' and hurt with them. See now their case. 1. Captives; and not only that, but 2. in prison. In prison; not above, but in the dungeon, the deepest, darkest, blindest hole there; no light, no sight at all. 3. And in the hole, with as many irons upon them, that they are even 'bruised' and sore with them. And tell me now, if these three together be not enough to break Manasses', or any man's heart, and to make him have *cor contritum* [a contrite heart] indeed.

They be; but what is this to us? This is no man's case here. No more was it any of theirs that were at Christ's sermon; yet Christ spake to the purpose, we may be sure. We may not then take it literally, as meant by the body: Christ meant no such captivity, dungeon, or irons. That He meant not such, is plain. He saith, He was sent to free captives, to open prisons; but He never set any captive free in His life, nor opened any gaol, in that sense, to let any prisoner forth. Another sense then we are to seek. Remember ye not, we began with the Spirit? the business the Spirit comes about is spiritual, not secular. So all these spiritually to be understood. As indeed they are all three applicable to the case of the Spirit, and a plain description of all our states out of Christ, and before He take us in hand.

1. There is captivity there, wherein men are held in slavery under sin and Satan, worse than that we now speak of. St Paul knew it, speaks of it, and when he hath so, crieth out, 'Wretched man that I am, who shall rid me of it?'[30] Verily, there is no Turk so hurries men, puts them to so base services, as sin doth her captives. Give me one that hath been in her captivity, and is got out of it, *et scit quod dico*, 'he can tell it is true I say.'

2. There is a prison too; not Manasses' prison. But ask David, who never came in any gaol, what he meant when he said, 'I am so fast in prison, as I know not how to get out.'[31] And that you may know what prison that was, he cries, 'O bring my soul out of prison!'[32] A prison there is then of the soul, no less than of the

---

[30] Romans 7:24
[31] 2 Chronicles 33:11; Psalm 88:8
[32] Psalm 142:7

58

body. In which prison were some of those that Christ preached here to; St Matthew saith, 'they sat in darkness and in the shadow of death',[33] even as men in the dungeon do.

3. There are chains too; – that also is the sinner's case, he is even 'tied with chains of his own sins',[34] saith Solomon, with 'the bonds of iniquity', St Peter;[35] which 'bonds' are they, David thanks God for breaking in sunder.[36] There need no other bonds we will say, if once we come to feel them. The galls that sin makes in the conscience, are 'the entering of the iron into our soul.'[37]

But you will say, We feel not these neither, no more than the former. No do? Take this for a rule: if Christ heal them that be broken-hearted, broken-hearted we behove to be ere He can heal us. He is *Medicus cordis* indeed; but it is *cordis contriti*. It is a condition ever annexed, this, to make us the more capable; and likewise a disposition it is, to make us the more curable. That same *pauperibus* before, and this *contritis* now, they limit Christ's cure, His cure and His commission both; and unless they be, or until they be, this Scripture is not, nor cannot be fulfilled in us. In our ears it may be, but in our hearts never.

That, as such as come to be healed by His Majesty are first searched, and after either put by or admitted as cause is; so there would be a scrutiny of such as make toward Christ. What, are you poor? Poor in spirit? – for the purse it skills not. No, but *dicis quia dives*, 'in good case':[38] Christ is not for you then, He is sent to the poor. What, is your heart broken? No, but heart-whole, 'a heart as brawn':[39] – then are you not for this cure. In all Christ's dispensatory, there is not a medicine for such a heart, 'a heart like brawn', that is hard and unyielding.

Christ Himself seems to give this item, when He applies it after. 'Many widows', 'many lepers', saith He, and so many sinners. 'Elias sent to none but the poor widow of Sarepta'; 'Eliseus healed none, but only Naaman,'[40] after his spirit came down, was broken. No more doth Christ, but such as are of a contrite heart.

---

[33] Matthew 4:16
[34] Proverbs 5:22
[35] Acts 8:23
[36] Psalm 116:16

[37] Psalm 105:18
[38] Revelation 3:17
[39] Psalm 119:70
[40] Luke 4:25-27

Verily, the case as before we set it down, is the sinner's case, feel he it, feel he it not. But if any be so benumbed, as he is not sensible of this; so blind as, dungeon or no dungeon, all is one to him; if any have this same *scirrhum cordis* [hardness of heart], that makes him past feeling, it is no good sign; but it may be, our hour is not yet come, our cure is yet behind. But if it should so continue, and never be otherwise, then were it a very evil sign. For what is such a one's case but, as Solomon saith, 'as the ox that is led to the slaughter' without any sense, 'or the fool' that goes laughing when he is carried to be well whipped?[41] What case more pitiful?

You will say; we have no hammer, no worldly cross to break our hearts. It may be. That is Manasses' hammer, the common hammer indeed, but that is not King David's hammer, which I rather commend to you; the right hammer to do the feat, to work contrition in kind. The right is the sight of our own sins. And I will say this for it; that I never in my life saw any man brought so low with any worldly calamity, as I have with this sight. And these I speak of were not of the common sort, but men of spirit and valour, that durst have looked death in the face. Yet when God opened their eyes to see this sight, their hearts were broken, yea even ground to powder with it; contrite indeed.

And this is sure; if a man be not humbled with the sight of his sins, it is not all the crosses or losses in the world will humble him aright.

This is the right. And without any worldly cross this we might have, if we loved not so to absent ourselves from ourselves, to be even *fugitivi cordis*, to run away from our own hearts, be ever abroad, never within; if we would but sometimes *redire ad cor*,[42] return home thither and descend into ourselves; sadly and seriously to bethink us of them, and the danger we are in by them; this might be had, and this would be had if it might be. If not, in default of this (no remedy) the common hammer must come; and God send us Manasses' hammer to break it; some bodily sickness, some worldly affliction, to send us home into ourselves!

---

41 Proverbs 7:22   42 Isaiah 46:8

60

But sure the Angel must come down and the water be stirred;[43] else we may preach long enough to uncontrite hearts, but no good will be done till then.

I have been too long in the cause; but the knowledge of the cause, in every disease, we reckon half the cure. To the healing now.

The word for heal in Esay, where this text is, signifies to bind up. The cure begins with ligature, the most proper cure for fractures. or aught that is broken. Nay, in wounds and all, as appeareth by the Samaritan.[44] The flux is so stayed, which, if it continue running on us still, in vain talk we of any healing. It is not begun till that stay and run no longer. The sin that Christ cures He binds up, He stays – to begin with. If He cover sin, it is with a plaister. He covers and cures together, both under one.

This word 'broken-hearted' the Hebrews take not as we do: we, broken for sin; they, broken off, or from sin. And we have the same phrase with us; to break one of the evil fashions or inclinations he hath been given to. So to break the heart. And so must it be broken, or ever it be whole. Both senses: either of them doth well, but both together best of all.

This done, now to the healing part. The heathen observed long since: Ψυχῆς νοσούσης εἰσὶν ἰατροὶ λόγοι, 'the soul's cure is by words';[45] and the Angel saith to Cornelius, of St Peter, 'He shall speak to thee words' by which thou and thy household shall be saved.[46]

And by no words sooner, than by the sound of good tidings. Good news is good physic sure, such the disease may be, and a good message a good medicine. There is power in it both ways. Good news hath healed, evil news hath killed many. The good news of Joseph's welfare, we see how it even 'revived' old Jacob.[47] And the evil of 'the Ark of God taken', it cost Eli his life.[48] Nothing works upon the heart more forcibly either way.

What are these news, and first how come they? By κηρύξαι [proclamation] they come; no secret-whispered news, from man

43 John 5:4
44 Luke 10:34
45 Aeschylus, *Prometheus Bound*, 1. 378

46 Acts 10:32
47 Genesis 45:27
48 I Samuel 4:18

to man in a corner; no flying news. They be proclaimed, these; so authentical. Proclaimed; and so they had need. For if our sins once appear in their right form, there is evil news certainly; let the devil alone with that, to proclaim them, to preach damnation to us. *Contraria curantur contrariis* [Things are cured by their opposites], we had need have some good proclaimed, to cure those of his.

Two proclamations here are, one in the neck of another. Of which the former, in the three branches of it, applieth in particular a remedy to the three former maladies, is the topic medicine, as it were; the latter is the panacea, makes them all perfectly whole and sound.

The first proclamation. To the captive first, that there is one at hand with a ransom to redeem him. This will make him a whole man.

2. To them in the dungeon; of one to draw them forth thence and make them ἀναβλέψαι, see the light again.

3. To them in chains; of one to strike off their bolts and loose them, to open the prison door and let them go; ἀποστεῖλαι, to make Apostles of them, and send them abroad into the wide world. It is the fruit of Christ's ἀπέσταλκε, this ἀποστεῖλαι Christ's Apostleship was, and is, to make such Apostles.

Now this is nothing but the very sum of the Gospel: 1. Of one coming with a ransom in one hand, to lay down for us the price of our redemption from Satan's captivity. 2. And with 'the keys of hell and death'[49] in the other. Keys of two sorts: 1. One to undo their fetters and loose them; 2. the other to open the dungeon and prison-door – both the dungeon of despair, and the prison of the law, and let them out of both. There can be no better news, nor kindlier physic in the world, 1. than word of redemption to captives; 2. than to see the light again, to them in the limbo; 3. than of enlargement to them in bands; but specially, than of a dismission from prison, dungeon, irons and all. And this is proclaimed here, and published by Christ in His Sermon at Nazareth; and was after performed and accomplished by Him, at His Passion in Jerusalem.

---

[49] Revelation 1:18

This is good news indeed, but here comes better. It is seconded with another proclamation, that makes up all. For in very deed, they that by the first proclamation were so released; for all that, and after all that, what were they but a sort of poor snakes turned out of the gaol, but have nothing to take to? Coming thither, they were turned out of all that ever they had. That their case, though it be less miserable, yet is miserable still; the *languor morbi* [weakness of illness] still hangs upon them.

We lack some restorative for that. Here comes now physic to cure that and make them perfectly well, a second κηρύξαι, that they shall be restored to all that ever they had. How so? For hark, here is 'the acceptable year', that is, a jubilee proclaimed. And then even of course they are, by force of the jubilee, so to be. The nature of the jubilee was so, you know. Then not only all bond set free, all prisons for debt set open; but beside, all were restored then to their former mortgaged, forfeited, or any ways aliened estates, in as ample manner as ever they had or held them at any time before.

A restitution *in integrum*, a re-investing them in what they were born to, or were any ways possessed of; that if they had sold themselves out of all, and lay in execution for huge sums, as it might be ten thousand talents, then all was quit, they came to all again, in as good case as ever they were in all their lives. There can be no more joyful news, no more cordial physic, than this. The year of jubilee? why that time so acceptable, so joyful, as it hath even given a denomination to joy itself. The height of joy is jubilee, the highest term to express it is *jubilate* [rejoice]; that goes beyond all the words of joy whatsoever.

And this comes well now; for the jubilee of the Law drawing to an end, and this very year being now the last, Christ's jubilee, the jubilee of the Gospel, came fitly to succeed. Wherein the primitive estate we had in Paradise, we are re-seized of anew. Not the same in specie, but as good, nay better. For if for the terrestrial Paradise by the flood destroyed we have a celestial, we have our own again, I trow, with advantage.

'A year' it is called, to keep the term still on foot that formerly it went by. Only this difference: the year there was a definite time, but here a definite is put for an indefinite. This year is more than twelve months. In this 'acceptable year' the Zodiack goes never about. On this day of salvation the sun never goes down. For in this the jubilee of the Gospel passeth that of the Law: that held but for a year, and no longer; but this is continual, lasts still. Which is plain, in that divers years after this of Christ's the Apostle speaks of it as still in *esse* [being]; even then makes this proclamation still, 'Behold this is the day, behold now is the acceptable time.'[50] Whereby we are given to understand that Christ's jubilee, though it began when Christ first preached this sermon, yet it ended not with the end of that year as did Aaron's, but was *Evangelium æternum*;[51] as also *perpetui jubilæi*, everlasting good news of a perpetual jubilee, that doth last and shall last as long as the Gospel shall be preached by Himself, or others sent by Him, to the end of the world, 'the time of restoring all things'.[52]

It is called 'acceptable', by the term of the benefit that happened on it, which was our acceptation. For then we and all mankind were made, not δεκτέοι, that is, 'acceptable', but as the word is, δεκτοὶ, that is, actually 'accepted', or received by God, out of Whose presence we were before cast. And being by Him so received, we did ourselves receive again, 'the earnest of our inheritance',[53] from which by means of the transgression we were before fallen.

There is much in this term 'accepting'. For when is one said to be accepted? Not when his ransom is paid, or the prison set open; not when he is pardoned his fault, or reconciled, or become friends; but when he is received with arms spread, as was the lost child in the Gospel, *ad stolam primam* [into his best robe] – as the term is, out of that place.[54] Three degrees there are in it: 1. Accepted to pardon – that is συγγνώμη. 2. Accepted to reconciliation, that is καταλλαγή. And further, 3. Accepted to repropitiation, that is ἱλασμὸς, to as good grace and favour as ever, even in the very fulness of it. They shew it by three distinct degrees in Absalom's receiving. 1. Pardoned he was, while he was yet in Geshur; 2. Reconciled, when he had to leave to come home to his

---

[50] 2 Corinthians 6:2
[51] Revelation 14:6
[52] Acts 3:21
[53] Ephesians 1:14
[54] Luke 15:20-22

own house; 3. Repropitiate, when he was admitted to the king's presence, and kissed him.[55] That made up all, then he had all again. And that is our very case.

Nay indeed, that is not all. It is more than so: δεκτὸς here is in the text of Esay, רצון ; and that imports more. For that word is ever turned by εὐδοκία, and that is Christ's own acceptation, 'In Whom I am well pleased',[56] and the very term of it. And he that is so accepted, I know not what he would have more.

This is the benefit that fell at this time; and for this that fell on the time, the time itself it fell on is, and cannot be but, acceptable; even *eo nomine* [on its own account], that at such a time such a benefit happened to us. And in this respect, it ever hath and ever shall be an acceptable welcome time, this, and holden as a high feast; like as the benefit is high, that befel us on it. *Festum*, 'a feast,' for the pardon; *Festum duplex* [doubled], for the reconciliation; *Festum magis duplex* [doubled again], for the being perfectly accepted to the favour of God, and by it re-accepting again our prime estate.

Nay last, it is called not only *Annus acceptus*, but *Annus Domini acceptus*, or *acceptus Domino*: not only, 'the acceptable year', but 'of the Lord', or 'to the Lord'; – for so the Hebrew reads it, with the sign of the dative, as if to God Himself it were so. And to Him so it is, and to His Holy Angels in Heaven so it is. For if the receiving any one contrite sinner, by repentance, be matter of joy to the whole court of Heaven[57] – the receiving of but one; what shall we think of the general receiving of the whole mass, which this day was effected?

Now if to Heaven, if to God Himself it be so; to earth, to us, shall it not be much more, whom much more it concerneth, I am sure? God getteth nothing by it; we do: He is not the better for it; we are: ever the receiver, than the giver. The giver more glory, but the receiver more joy. That if it be the joy of Heaven, it cannot be but the jubilee of the earth, even of the whole earth: *Jubilate Deo omnis terra*.[58]

The jubilee ever it began with no other sound, but even of a

---

[55] 2 Samuel 13:39, 14:23, 14:33
[56] Matthew 17:5
[57] Luke 15:10
[58] Psalm 66:1

cornet, made of the horns of a ram.[59] Of which horns they give no other reason but that it was so in reference to the horns of that 'ram that in the thicket was caught by the horns',[60] and sacrificed in Isaac's stead, even as Christ was in ours. To shew that all our jubilee hath relation to that special sacrifice, so plainly prefiguring that of Christ's. Which feast of jubilee began ever after the High-Priest had offered his sacrifice, and had been in the *Sancta sanctorum* [Holy of Holies]. As this jubilee of Christ also took place, from His entering into the holy places 'made without hands',[61] after His propitiatory sacrifice offered up for the quick and the dead, and for all yet unborn, at Easter. And it was the tenth day that; and this now is the tenth day since.

The memorial or mystery of which sacrifice of Christ in our stead is ever *caput lætitæ*, 'the top of our mirth', and the initiation of the joy of our jubilee. Like as *accipiam calicem salutaris*, our taking 'the cup of salvation',[62] is the memorial of our being accepted or received, and taken again to salvation. Wherewith, let us also crown this jubilee of ours. That so all the benefits of it may take hold of us; specially the redintegration of the favour of God, and the assurance or pledge of our restitution to those joys, and that jubilee, that only can give content to all our desires, when the time shall come of 'the restoring of all things'.[63]

---

[59] Leviticus 25:9; Joshua 6:4
[60] Genesis 22:13
[61] Hebrews 9:11

[62] Psalm 116:13
[63] Acts 3:21

A Sermon

PREACHED BEFORE

KING JAMES, AT WHITEHALL

on the Tenth of February, A.D. MDCXIX. Being Ash-Wednesday.

Joel ii: 12, 13.

*Therefore also now, saith the Lord, Turn you unto Me with all your
heart, and with fasting, and with weeping, and with mourning.*

*And rend your heart, and not your clothes, and turn unto the Lord
your God.*

*Nunc ergo dicit Dominus: convertimini ad Me in toto corde vestro,
in jejunio, et in fletu, et in planctu.*

*Et scindite corda vestra, et non vestimenta vestra, et convertimini ad
Dominum Deum vestrum.*

[*Therefore also now, saith the Lord, Turn ye even to Me with all your
heart, and with fasting, and with weeping, and with mourning.*

*And rend your heart, and not your garments, and turn unto the Lord
your God.*   Authorized Version]

For this time hath the Church made choice of this text. The time
wherein, howsoever we have dispensed with it all the year beside,
she should have us seriously to entend and make it our time of
turning to the Lord. And that 'now,' the first word of the text.

For she holds it not safe to leave us wholly to ourselves to take
any time it skills not when, lest we take none at all. 'Not now,'
saith Felix, 'but when I shall find a convenient time,'[1] and he
never found any; and many with him perish upon this 'not now'.
Take heed of ὅταν εὐκαιρήσω, 'when I shall find a convenient
time'; it undid Felix, that.

She hath found this same keeping of continual Sabbaths and
Fasts, this keeping the memory of Christ's birth and resurrection
all the year long hath done no good; hurt rather. So 'it hath
seemed good to the Holy Ghost'[2] and to her, to order there shall

---

[1] Acts 24:25   [2] Acts 15:28

be a solemn set return once in the year at least. And reason; for once a year all things turn. And that once is now at this time, for now at this time is the turning of the year. In Heaven, the sun in his equinoctial line, the zodiac and all the constellations in it, do now turn about to the first point. The earth and all her plants, after a dead winter, return to the first and best season of the year. The creatures, the fowls of the air, the swallow and the turtle, and the crane and the stork, 'know their seasons',[3] and make their just return at this time every year. Every thing now turning, that we also would make it our time to turn to God in.

Then because we are to turn *cum jejunio*, 'with fasting', and this day is known by the name of *caput jejunii*, 'the first day of Lent', it fits well as a welcome into this time – a time *lent* us as it were by God, set us by the Church, to make our turning in.

And besides the time 'now', the manner how is here also set down. For as it is true that repentance is the gift of God, *si quo modo det Deus pœnitentiam* [if God peradventure will give them repentance], saith the Apostle,[4] and we by prayer to seek it of Him that it would please Him to grant us true repentance, so it is true withal there is a 'doctrine of repentance from dead works', as saith the same Apostle,[5] and that is here taught us.

The Church turns us to these words here of the Prophet Joel, which, though they be a part of the Old Testament, yet for some special virtue in them as we are to believe, she hath caused them to be read for the Epistle of this day.

And surely had there been a plainer than this wherein the nature of true repentance had been more fully set forth, it behoveth us to think the Church inspired by the wisdom of God, would have looked it out for us against this time, the time sacred by her to our turning.

Again, that the Church carrying to her children the tender heart of a mother, if there were a more easy or gentle repentance than this of Joel, she would have chosen that rather. For this we are all bound to think, she takes no pleasure to make us sad, or to put upon us more than needs she must. Which in that she hath not,

---

[3] Jeremiah 8:7
[4] 2 Timothy 2:25

[5] Hebrews 6:1

we may well presume this of Joel is it she would have us hold our-selves to, and that this is, and is to be, the mould of our repentance.

I wot well, there is in this text somewhat of *sal terræ* [the salt of the earth],[6] something of the 'grain of mustard-seed' in the Gospel;[7] the points be such as we list not hear of. Fasting is *durus sermo*, an 'unwelcome point'[8] to flesh and blood; but as for weep-ing and mourning, and rending the heart, 'who can abide it?' The Prophet it seems foresaw we would say as much, and therefore he takes up the word before us. They be the words next before these, 'who can abide it?'[9] Abide what? These days? the absti-nence in them? No, but 'the great and fearful day of the Lord.' If you speak of not abiding, who can abide that? As if he should say, if you could abide that day when it comes, I would trouble you with none of these. But no abiding of that. Turn it away you may; turn it into a joyful day, by this turning to the Lord. Thus you may, and but thus you cannot. Now therefore you see how 'therefore' comes in. Here is our choice, one of them we must take. And better thus turn unto God in some of these little days, than be turned off by Him in 'that great day', to another manner weeping than this of Joel – even to 'weeping, and wailing, and gnashing of teeth.'[10] *Scientes igitur terrorem hunc*, 'knowing there-fore this fear',[11] and that upon this turning, *cardo vertitur*, the 'hinge turns' of our well or evil doing for ever, to be content to come to it and to turn the heathen man's[12] *non emam* into *emam tanti pœnitere* [I shall not buy, into, I shall buy such repentance]. To this turning then. Our charge is to preach to men, *non quæ volunt audire, sed quæ volunt audisse*, 'not what for the present they would hear, but what another day they would wish they had heard.'

Repentance itself is nothing else but *redire ad principia* [to return to first principles], 'a kind of circling,' to return to Him by repen-tance from Whom by sin we have turned away. And much after a circle is this text; begins with the word 'turn', and returns about to the same word again. Which circle consists, to use the Prophet's

---

[6] Matthew 5:13
[7] Matthew 13:31
[8] John 6:60
[9] Joel 2:11

[10] Matthew 8:12
[11] 2 Corinthians 5:11
[12] Demosthenes

own word, of two turnings; for twice he repeats this word, which two must needs be two different motions. 1. One, is to be done with the 'whole heart': 2. The other with it 'broken and rent'. So as one and the same it cannot be.

First, a 'turn', wherein we look forward to God, and with our 'whole heart' resolve to 'turn' to Him. Then a turn again, wherein we look backward to our sins wherein we have turned from God, and with beholding them our very heart breaketh. These two are two distinct, both in nature and names; one, conversion from sin; the other, contrition for sin. One resolving to amend that which is to come, the other reflecting and sorrowing for that which is past. One declining from evil to be done hereafter, the other sentencing itself for evil done heretofore. These two between them make up a complete repentance, or, to keep the word of the text, a perfect revolution.

And this and none other doth Joel teach the Jews, and this and none other doth Jonas teach the Gentiles. None other the Prophets, nor none other the Apostles; for St James comes just to this of Joel, enjoining sinners to 'cleanse their hands', and to 'purge their hearts', which is the former; and then withal, to 'change their laughter into mourning, and their joy into heaviness.'[13] Where πένθος and κατήφεια [mourning and heaviness], are as full for the New as *planctus* and *fletus* [weeping and mourning] are for the Old. These two; both these, and neither to spare; and we have not learned, we hold not, we teach not any other repentance. I speak it for this. There is a false imputation cast on us, that we should teach there goeth nothing to repentance but amendment of life; that these of fasting and the rest we let run by, as the waste of repentance; nay, that for fasting we do *indicere jejunium jejuniis*, 'we proclaim a fast from it', and teach a penitence with no penal thing in it. That therefore this text by name, and such other, we shun and shift, and dare not come near them. Not come near them? As near as we can by the grace of God, that the world may know, and all here bear witness, we teach and we press both.

Indeed, as Augustine well saith, *Aliud est quod docemus, aliud quod sustinemus*; 'What we are fain to bear with is one thing, what

---

[13] James 4:8-9

we preach and fain would persuade is another.' *Et væ tibi flumen moris humani,* saith he and we both, 'Woe to the strong current of a corrupt custom,' that hath taken such a head as, do what we can, it carries all headlong before it. But whatsoever we bear, this we teach though.

I forget myself. I intend to proceed as the words lie. 1. To 'turn', first; 2. and 'to God': 3. 'To God, with the heart'; 4. and 'with the whole heart'. Then the manner with these four; 1. 'Fasting'; 2. 'Weeping'; 3. 'Mourning'; 4. and a 'Rent heart'. Of which the two former are the body's task, 'fasting and weeping'; the two latter the soul's, 'mourning and rending the heart'. The former, 'mourning' the affection of sorrow; the latter 'rending', from anger or indignation, of both which affections repentance is compound and not of either alone. This for the manner how.

Then last for the time when; now to do it, 'Now therefore.'

Diversely and in sundry terms doth the Scripture set forth unto us the nature of repentance. Of renewing, as from a decay; of refining, as from a dross; of recovering, as from a malady; of cleansing, as from soil; of rising, as from a fall;[14] in no one, either for sense more full, or for use more often than in this of turning.

To 'turn' is a counsel properly to them that are out of their right way. For going on still and turning are motions opposite – both of them with reference to a way. For if the way be good, we are to hold on; if otherwise, to turn and take another.

Whether a way be good or no we principally pronounce by the end. If, saith Chrysostom, it be to a feast, good, though it be through a blind lane; if to execution, not good, though through the fairest street in the city. St Chrysostom was bidden to a marriage-dinner, was to go to it through divers lanes and alleys; crossing the high street, he met with one led through it to be executed; he told it his auditory, that *Non qua sed quo* [Not by which, but to which] was it.

If then our life be a 'way', as a 'way' it is termed in all writers, both holy and human, *via morum* no less than *via pedum* [a way of morals no less than a way of feet], the end of this way is to bring

---

[14] Hebrews 6:6; Jeremiah 6:29; Daniel 4:24; Jeremiah 8:4

us to our end, to our sovereign good which we call happiness. Which happiness not finding here but full of flaws, and of no lasting neither, we are set to seek it, and put in hope to find it with God, 'in Whose presence is the fulness of joy, and at Whose right hand pleasures for evermore.'[15]

From God then, as from the journey's end of our life, our way, we are never to turn our steps or our eyes, but with Enoch, as of him it is said, 'still to walk with God'[16] all our life long. Then should we never need to hear this *convertite*.

We are not so happy. There is one that maligneth we should go this way, or come to this end; and therefore to divert us holdeth out to us some pleasure, profit, or preferment; which to pursue, we must step out of the way, and so do full many times, even 'turn from God', to serve our own turns.

And this is the way of sin, which is a turning from God. When having in chase some trifling transitory, I wot not what, to follow it we even turn our backs upon God, and forsake the way of His commandments. And here now we first need His counsel of *convertite*.

For being entered into this way, yet we go too far in it; wisdom would we staid and were advised whither this way will carry us, and where we shall find ourselves at our journey's end. And reason we have to doubt; for after we once left our first way which was 'right', there takes us sometimes that same *singultus cordis*, as Abigail well calls it, 'a throbbing of the heart';[17] or, as the Apostle, certain 'accusing thoughts'[18] present themselves unto us which will not suffer us to go on quietly, our minds still misgiving us that we are wrong.

Besides, when any danger of death is near; nay, if we do but sadly think on it, a certain chillness takes us, and we cannot with any comfort think on our journey's end, and hear as it were a voice of one crying behind us, *Hæc est via*, That is not the way you have taken; 'This' that you have lost 'is your way, walk in it.'[19] Which voice if we hear not, it is long of the noise about us. If we

---

[15] Psalm 16:11
[16] Genesis 5:22
[17] 1 Samuel 25:31

[18] Romans 2:15
[19] Isaiah 30:21

would sometimes go aside into some retired place, or in the still of the night hearken after it, we might peradventure hear it.

A great blessing of God it is, for without it thousands would perish in the error of their life, and never return to their right way again. *Redite prævaricatores ad cor*, 'that sinners would turn to their own hearts.'[20] And this is the first degree to help us a little forward to this turning.

Being thus turned to our hearts we turn again and behold the τϱοχὸς γενέσεως, as St James termeth it, 'the wheel of our nature',[21] that it turneth apace, and turns off daily some, and them younger than we, and that within a while our turn will come that 'our breath also must go forth, and we turn again to our dust.'[22]

And when that is past, another of the Prophet, 'That Righteousness shall turn again to judgment':[23] Mercy that now sits in the throne, shall rise up and give place; Justice also shall have her turn. And then comes the last turn, *Convertentur peccatores in infernum*, 'the sinners shall be turned into hell, and all the people that forget' in time to turn unto 'God'.[24] There was wont to be a ceremony of giving ashes this day, to put us in mind of this *converteris*. I fear with the ceremony the substance is gone too. If that conversion into ashes be well thought on, it will help forward our turning.

This returning to our heart, the sad and serious bethinking us there of nature's conversion into dust, of sins into ashes – for ashes ever presuppose fire; that the wheel turns apace, and if we turn not the rather, these turnings may overtake us; God's spirit assisting may so work with us as we shall think Joel's counsel good, that if we have not been so happy as to keep the way, yet we be not so unhappy as not to turn again from a way, the issues whereof surely will not be good.

And would God these would serve to work it! If they will not, then must *conversus sum in ærumna dum configitur spina* [I be turned on the hard thorn that pierces me], 'some thorn in our

---

20 Isaiah 46:8
21 James 3:6
22 Psalm 146:4

23 Psalm 94:15
24 Psalm 9:17

73

sides,' some bodily or worldly grief must come and procure it.[25] But that is not to 'turn', but to be turned, and there is great odds between these two. As one thing it is 'to take up the cross', another to have it laid upon us.

To be turned I call, when by some cross of body or mind, as it were with a ring in our nose, we are brought about whether we will or no, to look how we have gone astray.

To turn I call, when the world ministereth unto us no cause of heaviness, all is *ex sententia* [to our liking]; yet even then the grace of God moving us, we set ourselves about, and representing those former conversions before us we work it out having from without no heavy accident to force us to it.

We condemn not *conversus sum in ærumna*; many are so turned, and God is gracious and rejects them not. But we commend this latter, when without wrench or screw we 'turn' of ourselves. And that man who being under no arrest, no bridle in his jaws, shall in the days of his peace resolve of a time to turn in and take it, that man hath great cause to rejoice and to rejoice before God. And thus much for *convertite*, or, if it may not be had, for *convertimini*.

'Turn', and 'turn to Me'; and He that saith it is God. Why, whither should we turn from sin but to God? Yes, we may be sure, it is not for nothing God setteth down this. In Jeremy it is more plain, 'If ye return, return to Me, saith the Lord';[26] which had been needless if we could turn to nothing else, were it not possible to find divers turnings, leaving one by-way to take another, from this extreme turn to that, and never to God at all. They that have been fleshly given, if they cease to be so, they turn; but if they become as worldly now as they were fleshly before, they turn not to God. They that from the dotage of superstition run into the phrensy of profaneness, they that from 'abhorring idols fall to commit sacrilege',[27] howsoever they turn, to God they turn not.

And this is even the *motus diurnus*, the common turning of the world, as Moses expresseth it, 'to add drunkenness to thirst',[28]

---

[25] Psalm 31:4 (Vulgate);
  2 Corinthians 12:7
[26] Jeremiah 4:1

[27] Romans 2:22
[28] Deuteronomy 29:19

from too little to too much, from one extreme to run into another. Would God it were not needful for me to make this note! But the true turn is *ad Me*, so from sin as to God. Else in very deed we turn from this sin to that sin, but not 'from sin'; or, to speak more properly, we turn sin, we turn not from sin, if we give over one evil way to take another.

'To Me', then, and 'with the heart'. And this also is needful. For, I know not how, but by some our conversion is conceived to be a turning of the brain only, by doting too much on the word *resipiscere* [to come to one's senses], as a matter merely mental. Where before thus and thus we thought, such and such positions we held, now we are of another mind than before, and there is our turning. This of Joel's is a matter of the heart sure. This? Nay, to say truth, where is conversion mentioned but it is in a manner attended with *in corde*? And so requireth not only an alteration of the mind but of the will, a change not of certain notions only in the head, but of the affections of the heart too. Else it is *vertigo capitis*, but not *conversio cordis* [turning of the head, but not conversion of the heart].

Neither doth this *in corde* stand only against the brain, but is commonly in opposition to the whole outward man. Else the heart may be fixed like a pole, and the body like a sphere turn round about it. Nay, heart and all must turn. Not the face for shame, or the feet for fear, but the heart for very hatred of sin also. Hypocrisy is a sin; being to turn from sin we are to turn from it also, and not have our body in the right way, and our heart still wandering in the by-paths of sin. But if we forbear the act which the eye of man beholdeth, to make a conscience of the thoughts too, for unto them also the eye of God pierceth. Thus it should be; else conversion it may be, but heart it hath none.

'With the heart', and 'with the whole heart'. As not to divide the heart from the body, so neither to divide the heart in itself. The devil, to hinder us from true turning, turns himself like Proteus into all shapes. First, turn not at all, you are well enough. If you will needs turn, turn whither you will, but not to God. If to God, leave your heart behind you, and turn and spare not. If with the heart, be it *in corde*, but not *in toto*, with some ends or fractions, with some few broken affections, but not entirely.

In modico, saith Agrippa, 'somewhat'; – there is a piece of the heart. *In modico et in toto*, saith St Paul, 'somewhat and altogether'; – there is 'the whole heart'.[29] For which cause, as if some converted with the brim or upper part only, doth the Psalm call for it *de profundis*, and the Prophet 'from the bottom of the heart'.[30]

To 'rend the heart' in this part is a fault, which is a virtue in the next. For it makes us have two hearts hovering as it were, and *in motu trepidationis* [in a state of alarm]; and fain we would let go sin, but not all that belongs to it; and turn we would from our evil way, but not from that which will bring us back to it again, the occasion, the object, the company, from which except we turn too we are in continual danger to leave our way again, and to turn back to our former folly, the second ever worse than the first.

When the heart is thus parcelled out, it is easily seen. See you one would play with fire and not be burned, 'touch pitch and not be defiled' with it, 'love peril, and not perish in it';[31] dallying with his conversion, turning 'like a door upon the hinges', open and shut, and shut and open again, with *vult et non vult*, 'he would, and yet he would not'? Be bold to say of that man, he is out of the compass of conversion; back again he will *ad volutabrum luti* [to his place in the mire].

And as easily it is seen, when one goes to his turning with his whole heart. He will come to his *quid faciemus?* [what shall we do?][32] Set him down what he should do, and he will do it. Not come near the place where sin dwelleth, refrain the wandering of his sense whereby sin is awaked, fulness and idleness whereof sin breedeth, but chiefly corrupt company whither sin resorteth. For conversion hath no greater enemy than conversing with such of whom our heart telleth us, there is neither faith nor fear of God in them. To all these he will come. Draw that man's apology, pronounce of him he is turned, and 'with his whole heart turned to God'. And so may we turn, and such may all our conversion be: 1. voluntary, without compulsion; 2. to God, without declining; 3. with the heart, not in speculation; with the whole heart entire, no purpose of recidivation!

---

[29] Acts 26: 28-29
[30] Psalm 130:1
[31] Ecclesiasticus 13:1, 3:27
[32] Luke 3:10

All this shall be done; we will 'turn with the heart, with the whole heart.' Is this all? No, here is a *cum* we must take with us, *cum jejunio*, 'with fasting'. Take heed of turning *cum* into *sine*, to say with it or without it we may turn well enough; since it is God Himself That to our turning joineth *jejunium*, we may not turn without it. Indeed, as I told you, this is but the half-turn. Hitherto we have but looked forward; we must also turn back our eye and reflect upon our sins past, be sorry for them, before our turning be as it should. The hemisphere of our sins not to be under the horizon clean out of our sight must ascend up, and we set them before us, and we testify by these four that follow how we like ourselves for committing of them.

I know we would have the sentence end here, the other stripped off, have the matter between our hearts and us, that there we may end it within, and no more ado; and there we should do well enough. But the Prophet tells us farther, or God Himself rather, for He it is that here speaketh, that our repentance is to be incorporate into the body no less than the sin was. Hers hath been the delight of sin, and she to bear a part of the penalty; that the heart within and the body without may both turn, since both have gone astray. It is a tax, a tribute, it hath pleased God to lay upon our sins and we must bear it.

I speak it for this. It is a world what strange conceits there are abroad touching this point. To the *animalis homo* [animal side of man] flesh and blood reveals a far more easy way not encumbered with any of these. To 'turn', and yet not lose a meal all the year long. and not shed a tear, and not 'rend' either 'heart or garment', and yet do full well. And with this conceit they pass their lives, and with this they pass out of their lives, as it seems resolved to put their souls in a venture, and to come to Heaven after their own fashion, or not come there at all. Change Joel into Jael, take a draught of milk out of her bottle, and wrap them warm, and lay them down, and never rise more.[33]

And that which is worse, they would not by their good-will have any other spoken of. For this is a disease of our nature; look

---

[33] Judges 4:18-21

how much we are of ourselves disposed to do, just so much and no more must be preached to us. For more than we have a liking to perform we cannot at any hand abide should be urged as needful. But these conceits must be left, or else we must tell Joel we can 'turn to God' without any of these. But it is not Joel, God it is that speaketh Who best knoweth what turning it is that pleaseth Him best; and Whom we must needs leave to prescribe the manner how He would have us to turn unto Him.

To speak after the manner of men, in very congruity when after a long aversion we are to turn and present ourselves before God, there would be a form set down how to behave ourselves, in what sort to perform it. This is it, how for our cheer, our countenance, how for our carriage every way. Very duty will teach us, if we will not break all the rules of decorum, we should do it suitably to such as have stood out in a long rebellion, and being in just disgrace for it are to approach the highest Majesty upon earth. Now would they being to return make a feast the same day they are to do it, with light merry hearts, with cheerful looks? and not rather with shame in their countenance, fear in their hearts, grief in their eyes? As they would, so let us. Still and ever remembering what the Prophet saith, *Magnus Rex Jehova*, 'God is a more high and mighty Prince than any on earth;'[34] stands on His State, will not be turn turned to, thus slightly, with or without it skills not. But we in our turning to come before Him all abashed and confounded in ourselves that for a trifle, a matter of nothing, certain carats of gain, a few minutes of delight – base creatures that we be! so, and so often, *sic et sic faciendo*, by such and such sins, have offended so presumptuously against so glorious a Majesty, so desperately against so omnipotent a Power, so unkindly against so sovereign a bounty of so gracious a God, and so kind and loving a Saviour.

To take them as they stand. 'Fasting'; which, were there nothing else but this, that the Church maketh this time of our return a time of fast, it shews plainly in her opinion how near these two are allied, how well they sort together. Which fast the

---

[34] Psalm 47:2; Malachi 1:4

Church prescribeth not only by way of regimen to keep the body low, that it may be a less mellow soil for the sins of the flesh, for this pertaineth to the former part so to prevent sin to come, but awards it as a chastisement for sin already past. For to be abridged, whether by others or by ourselves, of that which otherwise we might freely use, hath in it the nature of a punishment. They be the words of the Psalm, 'I wept and chastened myself with fasting';[35] 'chastened' himself – so a chastisement it is.

And thus preach we fasting; 1. Neither as the Physicians enjoin it in their aphorisms, to digest some former surfeit. 2. Nor as the Philosophers in their morals, to keep the sense subtile. 3. Nor as the States politic in their proclamations, to preserve the breed of cattle, or increase of strength by sea; but as the holy Prophets of God, as Joel straight after, we do *Sanctificare jejunium*,[36] prescribe it, and that to a religious end; even to chasten ourselves for sin by this forbearance. So no physical, philosophical, political, but a prophetical, yea an evangelical fast. For if in very sorrow we are to fast when 'the Bridegroom is taken away',[37] much more when we ourselves by our sins committed have been the cause of His taking, nay of His very driving away from us.

And must we then fast? Indeed we must, or get us a new Epistle for the day, and a new Gospel too. For as God here in the Epistle commands it, so Christ in the Gospel presupposeth it with His *cum jejunatis* [when ye fast],[38] taking it as granted we will fast. That sure fast we must, or else wipe out this *cum jejunio*, and that *cum jejunatis*, and tell God and Christ they are not well advised, we have found out a way beyond them to turn unto God without any fasting at all.

But how fast? To relieve all we may, when we speak of fasting, *humanum dicimus propter infirmitatem vestram* [we speak after the manner of men because of the infirmity of your flesh],[39] we intend not men's knees should 'grow weak with fasting'.[40] Two kinds of fasting we find in Scripture. 1. David's, who fasted,

---

[35] Psalm 69:10
[36] Joel 2:15
[37] Matthew 9:15

[38] Matthew 6:16
[39] Romans 6:19
[40] Psalm 109:24

'tasting neither bread' nor ought else 'till the sun was down',[41] no meat at all; – that is too hard. 2. What say you to Daniel's fast? 'He did eat and drink', but not *cibos desiderii*, 'no meats of delight', and namely ate no 'flesh'.[42] The Church, as an indulgent mother, mitigates all she may; enjoins not for fast that of David, and yet, *qui potest capere capiat* [He that is able to receive it, let him receive it][43] for all that; she only requires of us that other of Daniel, to forbear *cibos desiderii*, and 'flesh' is there expressly named – meats and drink provoking the appetite, full of nourishment, kindling the blood; content to sustain nature, and 'not purvey for the flesh to satisfy the lusts thereof.'[44] And thus by the grace of God we may, if not David's, yet Daniel's. For if David's we cannot, and Daniel's we list not, I know not what fast we will leave, for a third I find not.

And yet even this also doth the Church release to such as are in Timothy's case, have *crebras infirmitates* [often infirmities].[45] It is not the decay of nature, but the chastisement of sin she seeketh. But at this door all scape through; we are all weak and crazy when we would repent, but lusty and strong when to commit sin. Our physicians are easy to tell us, and we easy to believe any that will tell us, *propitius esto tibi*, 'favour yourself,' for it is not for you.[46]

Take heed, 'God is not mocked' Who would have sin chastened. Who sees I fear the pleasing of our appetite is the true cause, the not endangering our health is but a pretence. And He will not have His Ordinances thus dallied with, fast or loose. Said it must be that Joel here saith; 'Turn to God with fasting', or be ready to shew a good cause why, and to shew it to God. It is He here calls for it, the pen is but Joel's; He best knows what turning it is will serve our turn, will turn away *ira ventura* [the Wrath to come], which *Quis poterit sustinere*, 'Who is able to abide?'[47] And take this with you; when fasting and all is in, if it be, *Quis scit si convertatur Deus?* [Who knows if God will be turned?] If we leave what we please out, then it will be *Quis scit?* indeed.

---

[41] 2 Samuel 3:35
[42] Daniel 10:3
[43] Matthew 19:12
[44] Romans 13-14

[45] 1 Timothy 5:23
[46] Matthew 16:22
[47] Joel 2:11

The next point – and God send us well to discharge it! is 'weeping'. Can we not be dispensed with that neither, but we must weep too? Truly even in this point somewhat would be done too; else Joel will not be satisfied but call on us still. There is, saith the Psalm, a flagon provided by God of purpose for them;[48] therefore some would come, some few drops at least. Not as the Saints of old. No: *humanum dicimus* here too. Job's eyes 'poured forth tears to God'; David's eyes gushed out with water, he all to 'wet his pillow' with them; Mary Magdalene wept enough to have made a bath.[49] We urge not these. But if not pour out, not gush forth, *Nonne stillabit oculus noster*, saith Jeremy, 'Shall not our eye afford a drop or twain?'[50]

Stay a little, turn and look back upon our sins past; it may be, if we could get ourselves to do it in kind, if set them before us and look sadly, and not glance over them apace; think of them not once, but, as Ezekiah did, *recogitare*, 'think them over and over';[51] consider the motives, the base motives, and weigh the circumstances, the grievous circumstances, and tell over our many flittings, our often relapsing, our wretched continuing in them; it would set our sorrow in passion, it would bring down some – some would come; our bowels would turn, our repentings roll together, and lament we would the death of our soul as we do otherwhile the death of a friend, and for the unkindness we have shewed to God as for the unkindness we do that man sheweth us.

But this will ask time. It would not be posted through as our manner is – we have done straight. It is not a business of a few minutes; it will ask St Peter's χωρῆσαι, 'retired place', and St Paul's σχολάζειν, 'vacant time'.[52] It would ask a Nazarite's vow to do it as it should be done, even a sequestering ourselves for a time as they did; in other respects I grant, but among others for this also, even to perform to God a votive repentance. This I wish we would try. But we seek no place, we allow no time for it. Our other affairs take up so much as we can spare little or none for

---

[48] Psalm 56:8
[49] Job 16:20; Psalm 119:136
   Luke 7:38
[50] Jeremiah 13:17
[51] Isaiah 38:15
[52] 2 Peter 3:9; 1 Corinthians 7:5

this, which the time will come when we shall think it the weightiest affair of all.

And yet it may be, when all is done, none will come though. For who hath tears at command? Who can weep when he lists? I know it well, they be the overflowings of sorrow, not of every sorrow, but of the sensual parts; and being an act of the inferior parts, reason cannot command them at all times, they will not be had.

But if they will not, the Prophet hath here put an ἀντι-βαλλόμε-νον [alternative] in stead of it, for so do the Fathers all take it, 'Mourn'. If weep we cannot, mourn we can, and mourn we must. *Et vos non luxistis*, saith the Apostle;[53] he saith not, *et vos non flevistis*, 'and you have not wept', but 'and you have not mourned'; as if he should say, 'That you should have done at the least. Mourning they call the sorrow which reason itself can yield. In schools they term it, *Dolorem appretiativum*, 'valuing what should be', rating what the sins deserve though we have it not to lay down; yet what they deserve we should, and that we can. These and these sins I have committed, so many, so heinous, so oft iterate, so long lain in; these deserve to be bewailed even with tears of blood.

2. This we can; and this too wish with the Prophet, and so let us wish, 'O that my head were full of water, and my eyes fountains of tears',[54] to do as it should be done! This we can.

3. And pray we can, that He Which 'turneth the flint stone into a springing well',[55] would vouchsafe us, even as dry as flints, *gratiam lachrymarum* [the grace of tears], as the Fathers call it, some small portion of that grace to that end. Though weep we cannot, yet wish for it and pray for it we can.

4. And complain we can and bemoan ourselves as doth the Prophet, with a very little variation from him; 'My leanness, my leanness,' saith he, 'woe is me!'[56] 'My dryness, my dryness, may each of us say, woe is me! The transgressors have offended, the transgressors have grievously offended. Grievously offend we can, grievously lament we cannot, my dryness, my dryness, woe

---

[53] 1 Corinthians 5:2
[54] Jeremiah 9:1
[55] Psalm 114:8
[56] Isaiah 24:16

is me!' Nay, we need not vary, we may even let leanness alone, his own word. For dry and lean both is our sorrow, God wot: God help us! this mourn we can.

5. And lastly, this we can; even humbly beseech our merciful God and Father, in default of ours to accept of the 'strong crying and bitter tears which in the days of His flesh His blessed Son in great agony shed for us';[57] for us I say that should, but are not able to do the like for ourselves, that what is wanting in ours may be supplied from thence. These by the grace of God we may do in discharge of this point. These let us do, and it will be accepted.

And so now to the last, 'Rend your hearts' – you see first and last, to the heart we come. For indeed a meal may be missed, a tear or two let fall, and the heart not affected for all that. Esau wept, Ahab gave over his meat, their hearts both swelling and apostumate still.[58] To shew, that though these be requisite all, yet that the passion of the heart is *caput pœnitentiæ* [the main part of repentance]; to the heart He cometh again always, to verify that; in both and in all, *quod cor non facit non fit*, 'if it be not done with the heart, if the heart do it not, nothing is done.' As in conversion the purpose of amendment must proceed from the heart, so in our contrition, the sorrow, the anger, for our turning away, must pierce to the heart; some *cardiaque* passion to be, the heart to suffer.

And what must it suffer? Contrition – it should even *conteri*, be 'ground to powder'. 'A contrite heart', it should be? If not that, not *contritum*, yet *cor confractum*, 'a broken heart', broken in pieces, though not so small.[59] If neither of these, yet with this qualifying here, *cor conscissum*, with some rent, or cleft. *Solutio continui*, somewhat there is to be opened; not only that the apostumate matter may breathe forth, but much more, which is the proper of this part, that feeling the smart there we may say, and say it with feeling, *quod malum et amarum*, that an 'evil thing it is and a bitter, to have turned away and forsaken the Lord.'[60] Some such thing is the heart to feel, or else nothing is done.

Now this 'rending', if we mark it well, doth not so properly

[57] Hebrews 5:7
[58] Genesis 27:38; 1 Kings 21:27
[59] Psalm 51:17
[60] Jeremiah 2:19

pertain to the passion of sorrow, but rather to another, even to that of anger. 'Their hearts rend for anger,' it is said.[61] And it easily appeareth, for we use violence to that we rend. Ephraim's smiting his thigh, the Publican his breast,[62] both the acts of anger rather than heaviness. The Apostle puts into his repentance indignation and revenge, no less than he doth sorrow.[63]

To say truth, they are to go together. Sorrow, if it have no power to revenge, grows to be but a heavy dull passion; but if it have power, indignation and it go together. One cannot truly be said to be grieved with the thing done, but he must be angry with the doer; and we, if we be sorry indeed for our sin, will be angry with the sinner. So was Job: 'Therefore I abhor myself.'[64] 'Myself', saith he; not so much the sin, which was done and past, and so incapable of anger, as myself for the sin. Which if it be indignation indeed in us, and not a gentle word, will seek revenge some way or other: 'Grind to powder, break in pieces', at least make a 'rent'. *Contritio, confractio, conscissio, compunctio*, somewhat it will be.

But when we return to enquire, whether and which of these two acts hath in it the very true essence of repentance? In conversion I find it not. Why? For 'after I converted, I repented,' saith Jeremy;[65] and *Nihil prius aut posterius seipso*, 'nothing is after itself.' Conversion then is not it. And when we seek for it in this latter, first, in sorrow it is not; Why? For *tristitia operatur pœnitentiam* [godly sorrow works repentance], saith the Apostle[66] – mark that *operatur*, 'works' it; therefore is not it, for *nihil sui causa* [nothing is its own cause]. It remains then of force, that it is in this now of indignation. So that now, and not before, are we come to the essence of it indeed. And set down this; that ἀγανάκτησις, 'indignation', is the essential passion, and ἐκδίκησις, 'revenge', or this 'rending' here, the principal and most proper act of a true turning unto God.[67]

Now if you ask how or which way we can come to make a rent

---

[61] Acts 7:54
[62] Jeremiah 31:19; Luke 18:13
[63] 2 Corinthians 7:11
[64] Job 42:6
[65] Jeremiah 31:19
[66] 2 Corinthians 7:10
[67] 2 Corinthians 7:11

in the heart, since no hand may touch it and we live? the meaning is not literal; but that the heart by reflecting on itself is able to make such an impression on it as the Prophet may well call 'a rent in the heart'. As first, even by good moral respects, wherewith the very heathen set themselves in passion against vice. That it is a brutish thing, so against the nobleness of reason; that a shameful, so against public honesty; that ignominious, so against our credit and good name; that pernicious, as shutting us out of Heaven whither we would come, the greatest loss and *pœna damni* [punishment of the damned], and pressing us down to hell which we fainest would fly, the greatest torment and *pœna sensus* [punishment of the senses]; for even the heathen believed the joys and pains of another world. And yet we for all this so evil advised as to commit it.

But these are but κατ' ἄνθρωπον, 'drawn from man;' the Christian man's is to be ἐις Θεὸν, his eye to God. Who with great indignation cannot but abhor himself for the manifold indignities offered to God thereby? To the law of His justice, to the awe of His Majesty, the reverend regard of His Presence, the dread of His power, the long-suffering of His love; that being a creature of vile and brittle consistence he hath not sticked for some lying vanity, some trifling pleasure or pelting profit, to offend so many ways at once all odious in themselves and able to make a rent in any heart that shall weigh them aright.

Sure if we take the impression right, so God may work with us, as these may work in us, a just indignation, which, if once it be in fervour, what the hand can come to it will smite, and would the heart also, if it could reach it. And if it be in kind, it will award the body to fast, and the mind to spend some time in these meditations. And this is the act of 'rending' as the Prophet, of 'revenge' as the Apostle;[68] and these two between them both, in Joel and in Paul, make up the full power and *consummatum est* [it is finished] of our conversion and contrition both.

It remains that we set not the Church to teach us that which we never mean to learn, but that we intend and endeavour to do as we have been taught.

---

[68] Joel 2:13; 2 Corinthians 7:11

And to do it now. For, as in a circle, I return to the first word 'now', which giveth us our time when we should enter our first degree; – 'now therefore'. And when all is done we shall have somewhat to do to bring this to a *nunc*, to a time present. But besides that 'now' at this time, it is the time that all things turn, now is the only sure part of our time. That which is past is come and gone, that which is to come may peradventure never come. Till to-morrow, till this evening, till an hour hence, we have no assurance. 'Now therefore.' Or if not 'now', as near 'now', with as little distance from it as may be; if not this day, this time now ensuing.

For though no time be amiss to turn in, yet seeing many times go over our heads, and still we cannot find a time to do it in, the Church as I said willing to reduce the diffusedness of our repentance at large to the certainty of some one set time, hath placed this 'now' upon the time now begun, and commends it to us for the time of our turning to God.

And we by a kind of form which we perform, by the altering of our diet to a less desireful, by oftener resort hither to sermons than at other times, every week twice – these make as if we did agree, seem in a manner to promise as if we would perform somewhat 'now' that we have not all the year before.

Sure the Christian Church ever looked otherwise, had another manner face: going in the street you should have seen by men's countenances what time of the year it was – more grave, more composed, than at other times.

Perform it then; and when our turn is done God shall begin His, *et pœnitentiam suam gratificabitur nostræ*, 'our repentance shall beget His.' If we turn from the evil we have done, He will turn from us the evil that should have been done to us. Where there was Commination read with many curses, He shall turn them away and instead of them shall leave a blessing behind Him. We shall turn His very style, which at first was *ad Me* [to Me], and in the end is *ad Dominum Deum vestrum* [to the Lord your God]; and so make a change in Him.

In nullo detrimentum patiemini, saith the Apostle, 'we shall be no losers by it'.[69] A less sorrow shall turn away a greater by a great

---

[69] 2 Corinthians 7:9

deal. Weigh the endless sorrow we shall escape by it – it admits no comparison. The contristation is but πρὸς ὥραν, saith he, 'for an hour',[70] the consolation is 'for ever and ever'.

To this *lugentes*, there belongeth a *beati*, 'blessed they that thus mourn.' To this 'hunger and thirst', a *saturabimini* [they shall be filled].[71] It is so set by the Church, the time of it, that our Lent shall end with an Easter, the highest and most solemn feast in the year, the memory of Christ's rising, and the pledge of our blessed and joyful resurrection. To which, &c.

---

[70] 2 Corinthians 7:8   [71] Matthew 5:4-6

A Sermon

PREACHED BEFORE THE

KING'S MAJESTY, AT WHITEHALL

on the Sixteenth of April, A.D. MDCXX. Being Easter-Day.

John xx: 11-17.

But Mary stood by the sepulchre weeping; and as she wept, she stooped, and looked into the sepulchre,

And saw two Angels in white, sitting, the one at the head, the other at the feet, where the Body of Jesus had lain.

And they said to her, Woman, why weepest thou? She said to them, They have taken away my Lord, and I know not where they have laid Him.

When she had thus said, she turned herself about, and saw Jesus standing, and knew not that it was Jesus.

Jesus saith to her, Woman, why weepest thou? Whom seekest thou? She, supposing He had been the gardener, said to Him, Sir, if thou have borne Him hence, tell me where thou hast laid Him, and I will take Him thence.

Jesus saith to her, Mary. She turned herself, and said to Him, Rabboni, that is to say, Master.

Jesus said to her, Touch Me not; for I am not yet ascended to My Father: but go to My brethren, and say to them, I ascend to My Father, and to your Father, and to My God and your God.

[Maria autem stabat ad monumentum foris, plorans: Dum ergo fleret, inclinavit se, et prospexit in monumentum;

Et vidit duos Angelos in albis, sedentes, unum ad caput, et unum ad pedes, ubi positum fuerat corpus Jesu.

Dicunt ei illi, Mulier, quid ploras? Dicit eis, Quia tulerunt Dominum meum, et nescio ubi posuerunt Eum.

Hæc cum dixisset, conversa est retrorsum, et vidit Jesum stantem, et non sciebat quia Jesus est.

Dicit ei Jesus, Mulier, quid ploras? quem quæris? Illa existimans quia hortulanus esset, dicit ei, Domine, si tu sustulisti Eum, dicito mihi ubi posuisti Eum, et ego Eum tollam.

Dicit ei Jesus, Maria. Conversa illa, dicit Ei, Rabboni, quod dicitur
Magister.
Dicit ei Jesus, Noli Me tangere, nondum enim ascendi ad Patrem
Meum: vade autem ad fratres meos, et dic eis, Ascendo ad Patrem
Meum, et Patrem vestrum, Deum Meum, et Deum vestrum.
Latin Vulg.]

[*But Mary stood without at the sepulchre weeping; and as she wept,*
she stooped down and looked into the sepulchre,
And seeth two Angels in white, sitting, the one at the head, and the
other at the feet, where the body of Jesus had lain.
And they said unto her, Woman, why weepest thou? She saith unto
them, Because they have taken away my Lord, and I know not
where they have laid Him.
And when she had thus said, she turned herself back, and saw Jesus
standing, and knew not that it was Jesus.
Jesus saith unto her, Woman why weepest thou? whom seekest thou?
She, supposing Him to be the gardener, saith unto Him, Sir, if
thou have borne Him hence, tell me where thou hast laid Him,
and I will take Him away.
Jesus saith unto her, Mary. She turned herself, and saith unto Him,
Rabboni, which is to say, Master.
Jesus saith unto her, Touch Me not; for I am not yet ascended to My
Father: but go to My brethren, and say unto them, I ascend unto
My Father and your Father, and to My God and your God.
Authorized Version]

This last verse was not touched.

It is Easter-day abroad, and it is so in the text. We keep Solomon's
rule, *Verbum diei in die suo* [The word of the day on the day itself][1]
For all this I have read, is nothing else but a report of Christ's
rising, and of His appearing this Easter-day morning, His very
first appearing of all. St Mark is express for it, that Christ was no
sooner risen this day but 'He appeared first of all to Mary Magdalene';[2] which first appearing of His is here by St John extended,
and set down at large.

---

[1] 1 Kings 8:59   [2] Mark 16:9

The sum of it is, 1. The seeking Christ dead; 2. The finding Him alive.

The manner of it is, That Mary Magdalene staying still by the sepulchre, first she saw a vision of Angels; and after, she saw Christ Himself. Saw Him, and was herself made an Angel by Him, a good Angel to carry the Evangel, the first good and joyful tidings of His rising again from the dead. And this was a great honour, all considered, to serve in an Angel's place. To do that at His resurrection, His second birth, that at His first birth an Angel did. An Angel first published that, Mary Magdalene brought first notice of this. As he to the shepherds, so she to the Apostles, the Pastors of Christ's flock, by them to be spread abroad to the ends of the world.

To look a little into it. 1. Mary is the name of a woman; 2. Mary Magdalene of a sinful woman.

That to a woman first – it agreeth well to make even with Eve; that as by a woman came the first news of death, so by a woman also might come the first notice of the Resurrection from the dead. And the place fits well, for in a garden they came both.

That to a sinful woman first – that also agrees well. To her first that most needed it; most needed it, and so first sought it. And it agrees well, He be first found of her that first sought Him; even in that respect she was to be respected.

In which two there is opened unto us 'a gate of hope',[3] two great leaves, as it were; one, that no infirmity of sex – for a woman we see; the other, that no enormity of sin – for a sinful woman, one that had the blemish that she went under the common name of *peccatrix* [sinner],[4] as notorious and famous in that kind; that neither of these shall debar any to have their part in Christ and in His resurrection; any, that shall seek Him in such sort as she did. For either of these *non obstante*, nay notwithstanding both these, she had the happiness to see His Angels – and that was no small favour; to see Christ Himself, and that first of all, before all others to see and salute Him; and to receive a commission from Him of *vade et dic*, to 'go and tell', that is as it were to be an Apostle, and

_____

[3] Hosea 2:15   [4] Luke 7:37

that to the Apostles themselves, to bring them the first good news of Christ's rising again.

There are three parties that take up the whole text, and if I should divide it, I would make those three parties the three parts; I. Mary Magdalene, II. the Angels, III. and Christ our Saviour.

Mary Magdalene begins her part in the first verse, but she goes along through them all.

Then the Angels' part in the two verses next. 1. Their appearing, 2. and their speech to her; appearing in the twelfth, speech in the thirteenth.

And last, Christ's part in all the rest. 1. His appearing, 2. and speech likewise. Appearing first, unknown, in the fourteenth, and His speech then in the fifteenth.

After, His appearing and speech again, being known, in the sixteenth and seventeenth. 1. Forbidding her, *mane et tange*, to stay and to touch; 2. and bidding her, *vade et dic*, to get her quickly to His brethren, and tell them His resurrection was past, for *ascendo*, He was taking thought for His Ascension, and preparing for that. Thus lieth the order and the parts.

The use will be, that we in our seeking carry ourselves as she did; – and so may we have the happiness that she had to find Christ, as He is now to be found in the virtue of His resurrection!

Ver. 11. 'But Mary stood by the Sepulchre weeping, and as she wept she stooped, and looked into the Sepulchre.'

Of the favours vouchsafed this same *felix peccatrix* [happy sinner], as the Fathers term her, this day; 1. To see but Christ's Angels, 2. To see Christ at all, 3. To see Him first of all, 4. But more than all these, to be employed by Him in so heavenly an errand, reason we can render none that helped her to these, but that which in a place Christ Himself renders, *Quia dilexit multum*, 'because she loved much'.[5]

'She loved much'; we cannot say, She believed much; for by her *sustulerunt* [they have taken him away] thrice repeated, the second, thirteenth, fifteenth verses,[6] it seems she believed no more than just as much as the High Priests would have had the world believe, that 'he was taken away by night.'

---

[5] Luke 7:47   [7] John 20:2, 13, 15

Defectus fidei non est negandus, affectus amoris non est vituperandus: it is Origen;[7] 'We cannot commend her faith, her love we cannot but commend,' and so do – commend it in her, commend it to you. Much it was, and much good proof gave she of it. Before, to Him living; now, to Him dead. To Him dead, there are divers: 1. She was last at His cross, and first at His grave; 2. Stayed longest there, was soonest here; 3. Could not rest till she were up to seek Him; 4. Sought Him while it was yet dark, before she had light to seek Him by.[8]

But to take her as we find her in the text, and to look no whither else. There are in the text no less than ten, all arguments of her great love; all as it were a commentary upon *dilexit multum*. And even in this first verse there are five of them.

The first in these words, *stabat juxta monumentum*, that 'she stood by the grave', a place where faint love loves not to stand. Bring Him to the grave, and lay Him in the grave, and there leave Him; but come no more at it, nor stand not long by it. Stand by Him while He is alive – so did many; stand, and go, and sit by Him. But *stans juxta monumentum*, stand by Him dead; Mary Magdalene, she did it, and she only did it, and none but she. *Amor stans juxta monumentum*.

The next in these, *Maria autem stabat*, 'But Mary stood'. In the *autem*, the 'but' – that helps us to another. 'But Mary stood', that is as much to say as, Others did not, 'but' she did. Peter and John were there but even now. Thither they came, but not finding Him, away they went.[9] They went, but Mary went not, she stood still. Their going away commends her staying behind. To the grave she came before them, from the grave she went to tell them, to the grave she returns with them, at the grave she stays behind them. *Fortior eam figebat affectus*, saith Augustine,[10] 'a stronger affection fixed her'; so fixed her that she had not the power to remove thence. Go who would, she would not, but stay still. To stay, while others do so, while company stays, that is the world's love; but Peter is gone, and John too; all are gone,

---

[7] Origen, *Homily on St Mary Magdalene*
[8] Matthew 28:1
[9] John 20:3-10

[10] St Augustine, *Tractates on the Gospel of John*

and we left alone; then to stay is love, and constant love. *Amor manens aliis recedentibus*, 'love that when others shrink and give over, holds out still.'

The third in these, 'she stood, and she wept'; and not a tear or two, but she wept a good [deal] as we say, that the Angels, that Christ Himself pity her, and both of them the first thing they do, they ask her why she wept so. Both of them begin with that question. And in this is love. For if, when Christ stood at Lazarus' grave's side and wept, the Jews said, 'See, how He loved him!'[11] may not we say the very same, when Mary stood at Christ's grave and wept, See, how she loved Him! Whose presence she wished for, His miss she wept for; Whom she dearly loved while she had Him, she bitterly bewailed when she lost Him. *Amor amare flens*, 'love running down the cheeks'.

The fourth in these, 'And as she wept, she stooped, and looked in' ever and anon. That is, she did so weep as she did seek withal. Weeping without seeking, is but to small purpose. But her weeping hindered not her seeking, her sorrow dulled not her diligence. And diligence is a character of love, comes from the same root, *dilectio* [love] and *diligentia* [diligence] from *diligo* [I love], both. *Amor diligentiam diligens* [Love loving diligence].

To seek, is one thing; not to give over seeking, is another. For I ask, why should she now look in? Peter and John had looked there before, nay had been in the grave, they. It makes no matter; she will not trust Peter's eyes, nor John's neither. But she herself had before this, looked in too. No force, she will not trust herself, she will suspect her own eyes, she will rather think she looked not well before, than leave off her looking. It is not enough for love to look in once. Thus we use, this is our manner when we seek a thing seriously; where we have sought already, there to seek again, thinking we did it not well, but if we look again better, we shall surely find it then. *Amor quærens ubi quæsivit*, love that never thinks it hath looked enough. These five.

And, by these five we may take measure of our love, and of the true *multum* [amount] of it. *Ut prosit nobis ejus stare, ejus plorare et*

---

[11] John 11:36

93

quærere, saith Origen, 'that her standing, her weeping, and seeking, we may take some good by them.'

I doubt ours will fall short. Stay by Him alive, that we can, *juxta mensam* [by his table]; but *juxta monumentum* [by his grave], who takes up His standing there? And our love it is dry-eyed, it cannot weep; it is stiff-jointed, it cannot stoop to seek. If it do, and we hit not on Him at first, away we go with Peter and John; we stay it not out with Mary Magdalene. A sign our love is little and light, and our seeking suitable, and so it is without success. We find not Christ – no marvel; but seek Him as she sought Him and we shall speed as she sped.

Ver. 16. 'And saw two Angels in white, sitting, the one at the head, the other at the feet, where the body of Jesus had lain.'

For what came of this? Thus staying by it, and thus looking in, again and again, though she saw not Christ at first, she sees His Angels. For so it pleased Christ to come by degrees, His Angels before Him. And it is no vulgar honour this, to see but an Angel; what would one of us give to see but the like sight?

We are now at the Angels' part, their appearing in this verse. There are four points in it: 1. Their place; 2. Their habit; 3. Their site; 4. and their order. 1. Place, in the grave; 2. Habit, in white; 3. site – they were sitting; 4. and their order in sitting, one at the head, the other at the feet.

The place. In the grave she saw them; and Angels in a grave, is a strange sight, a sight never seen before; not till Christ's body had been there, never till this day; this the first news of Angels in that place. For a grave is no place for Angels, one would think; for worms rather: blessed Angels, not but in a blessed place. But since Christ lay there, that place is blessed. There was a voice heard from Heaven, 'Blessed be the dead': 'Precious the death', 'Glorious the memory' now, 'of them that die in the Lord.'[12] And even this, that the Angels disdained not now to come thither, and to sit there, is an *auspicium* [augury] of a great change to ensue in the state of that place. *Quid gloriosius Angelo? quid vilius vermiculo?* saith Augustine. *Qui fuit vermiculorum locus, est et*

---

[12] Revelation 14:13; Psalm 116:15

Angelorum. 'That which was the place for worms, is become a place for Angels.'

Their habit. 'In white'. So were there divers of them, divers times this day, seen, 'in white' all; in that colour. It seems to be their Easter-day colour, for at this feast they all do their service in it. Their Easter-day colour, for it is the colour of the Resurrection. The state whereof when Christ would represent upon the Mount, 'His raiment was all white, no fuller in the earth could come near it.'[13] And our colour it shall be, when rising again we 'shall walk in white robes', and 'follow the Lamb whithersoever He goeth.'[14]

Heaven mourned on Good-Friday, the eclipse made all then in black. Easter-day it rejoiceth, Heaven and Angels, all in white. Solomon tells us, it is the colour of joy.[15] And that is the state of joy, and this the day of the first joyful tidings of it, with joy ever celebrated, even *in albis* [in white], eight days together, by them that found Christ.

'In white', and 'sitting'. As the colour of joy, so the situation of rest. So we say, Sit down, and rest. And so is the grave made, by this morning's work, a place of rest. Rest, not from our labours only – so do the beasts rest when they die; but as it is in the six-teenth Psalm, a Psalm of the Resurrection, a 'rest in hope'[16] – 'hope' of rising again, the members in the virtue of their Head Who this day is risen. So to enter into the 'rest', which yet 're-maineth' for the people of God',[17] even the Sabbath eternal.

'Sitting', and in this order 'sitting'; 'at the head one, at the feet another, where His body had lain.'

1. Which order may well refer to Christ Himself, Whose body was one true ark indeed, 'in which it pleased the Godhead to dwell bodily';[18] and is therefore here between two Angels, as was the ark, the type of it, 'between the two cherubims,'[19]

2. May also refer to Mary Magdalene. She had anointed His head, she had anointed His feet:[20] at these two places sit the two Angels, as it were to acknowledge so much for her sake.

---

[13] Mark 9:3
[14] Revelations 3:4; Revelations 14:4
[15] Ecclesiastes 9:8
[16] Psalm 16:9
[17] Hebrews 4:9
[18] Colossians 2:9
[19] Exodus 25:22
[20] Matthew 26:7; John 12:3

3. In mystery, they refer it thus. Because *caput Christi Deus*, 'the Godhead is the head of Christ',[21] and His feet which the serpent did bruise,[22] His manhood; that either of these hath his Angel. That to Christ man no less than to Christ God, the Angels do now their service. *In principio erat Verbum* [In the beginning was the Word], His Godhead; there, an Angel. *Verbum caro factum* [The Word was made flesh], his manhood; there, another.[23] 'And let all the Angels of God worship Him'[24] in both. Even in His manhood, at His cradle the head of it, a choir of Angels;[25] at His grave, the feet of it, Angels likewise.

4. And lastly, for our comfort thus. That henceforth even such shall our graves be, if we be so happy as to 'have our parts in the first resurrection',[26] which is of the soul from sin. We shall go to our graves in white, in the comfort and colour of hope, lie between two Angels there; they guard our bodies dead, and present them alive again at the Resurrection.

1. Yet before we leave them, to learn somewhat of the Angels; specially, of 'the Angel that sat at the feet'. That between them there was no striving for places. He that 'sat at the feet', as well content with his place as he that 'at the head'. We to be so by their example. For with us, both the Angels would have been 'at the head', never an one 'at the feet'; with us none would be at the feet by his good will, head-Angels all.

2. Again, from them both. That inasmuch as the head ever stands for the beginning, and the feet for the end, that we be careful that our beginnings only be not glorious – O an angel at the head in any wise – but that we look to the feet, there be another there too. *Ne turpiter atrum desinat*,[27] 'that it end not in a black Angel,' that began in a white. And this for the Angels' appearing.

Ver. 13. 'And they said to her, Woman why weepest thou? She said to them, They have taken away my Lord, and I know not where they have laid Him.'

Now to their speech. It was not a dumb show this, a bare

---

[21] 1 Corinthians 11:3
[22] Genesis 3:15
[23] John 1:1, 14
[24] Hebrews 1:6
[25] Luke 2:13
[26] Revelation 20:6
[27] Horace, *Art of Poetry*, 11. 3-4

apparition, and so vanished away. It was *visio et vox*, 'a vocal vision'. Here is a dialogue too, the Angels speak to her.

And they ask her, *Quid ploras?* Why she wept, what cause she had to weep. They mean she had none, as indeed no more she had. All was in error, *piæ lachrymæ sed cæcæ*, 'tears of grief but false grief', imagining that to be that was not, Him to be dead that was alive. She weeps, because she found the grave empty, which God forbid she should have found full, for then Christ must have been dead still, and so no Resurrection.

And this case of Mary Magdalene's is our case oftentimes. In the error of our conceit to weep, where we have no cause; to joy, where we have as little. Where we should, where we have cause to joy, we weep; and where to weep, we joy. Our *ploras* hath never a *quid*. False joys and false sorrows, false hopes and false fears this life of ours is full of – God help us!

Now because she erred, they ask her the cause, that she alleging it they may take it away, and shew it to be no cause. As the clench, *a non causâ pro causâ* [a causeless because], makes foul rule among us, beguiles us all our life long.

Will ye hear her answer to 'Why weep you?' why? *sustulerunt*, that was her cause, her Lord was gone, was 'taken away'.

And a good cause it had been, if it had been true. Any have cause to grieve that have lost, lost a good Lord, so good and gracious a Lord as He had been to her.

But that is not all; a worse matter, a greater grief than that. When one dieth, we reckon him taken away; that is one kind of taking away. But His dead body is left, so all is not taken from us; that was not her case. For in saying, 'her Lord', she means not her Lord alive – that is not it; she means not they had slain Him, they had taken away His life – she had wept her fill for that already. But 'her Lord', that is, His dead body. For though His life was gone, yet His body was left. And that was all she now had left of Him that she calls her Lord, and that 'they had taken away' from her too. A poor one it was, yet some comfort it was to her, to have even that left her to visit, to anoint, to do other offices of love, even to that. *Etiam viso cadavere recalescit amor*, at the sight even of that will love revive, it will fetch life of love again. But now here is her case; that is gone and all, and nothing but an empty grave now left to stand by. That St Augustine saith well, *sublatus de monumento* [taken away from the sepulchre] grieved her more than *occisus in ligno* [killed on the Cross], for then something yet was left; now nothing at all. Right *sustulerunt*, taken away quite and clean.

And thirdly, her *nescio ubi* [I know not where]. For though He be taken away, it is some comfort yet, if we know where to fetch Him again. But here, He is gone without all hope of recovery or getting again. For 'they' – but she knew not who, 'had carried Him' she knew not whither; 'laid Him', she knew not where; there to do to Him, she knew not what. So that now she knew not whither to go, to find any comfort. It was *nescio ubi* with her right. Put all these together, His life taken away, His body taken away, and carried no man knows whither; and do they ask why she wept? or can any blame her for it?

The truth is, none had 'taken away her Lord' for all this; for all this while her Lord was well, was as she would have had Him, alive and safe. He went away of Himself, none carried Him thence. What of that? *Non credens suscitatum, credidit sublatum*, 'for want of belief He was risen, she believed He was carried away.' She erred in so believing; there was error in her love, but there was love in her error too.

And give me leave to lay out three more arguments of her love, out of this verse, to make up eight, towards the making up of her *multum* [account].

The very title she gives Him, of *Dominum meum*, is one; 'My Lord', that she gives Him that term. For it shews her love and respect was no whit abated by the scandal of His death. It was a most opprobrious, ignominious, shameful death He suffered; such, as in the eyes of the world any would have been ashamed to own Him, or say of Him, *Meum*; but any would have been afraid to honour Him with that title, to style Him *Dominum*. She was neither. *Meum*, for hers; *Dominum meum*, for her Lord she acknowledgeth Him, is neither ashamed nor afraid to continue that title still. *Amor scandalo non scandalizatus* [Love is not scandalized by scandal].

Another, which I take to be far beyond this, That she having looked into the grave a little before, and seen never an Angel there, and of a sudden looking in now and seeing two, a sight able to have amazed any, any but her, it moves her not at all. The suddenness, the strangeness, the gloriousness of the sight, yea, even of Angels, move her not at all. She seems to have no sense of it, and so to be in a kind of extacy all the while. *Domine, propter Te est extra se* [Lord, to be beside Thee is to be outside oneself], saith Bernard. *Amor extasin patiens* [Love can bear ecstasy].

And thirdly, as that strange sight affected her not a whit, so neither did their comfortable speech work with her at all. Comfortable I call it, for they that ask the cause why, 'why weep you?' shew they would remove it if it lay in them. Neither of these did or could move her, or make her once leave her weeping – she wept on still: Christ will ask her, *quid ploras?* [why weepest thou?] by and by again. If she find an Angel, if she find not her Lord, it will not serve. She had rather find His dead body, than them in all their glory. No man in earth, no Angel in Heaven can comfort her; none but He that is taken away, Christ, and none but Christ; and till she find Him again, her soul refuseth all manner comfort, yea even from Heaven, even from the Angels themselves; these three. *Amor super amissum renuens consolari* [Love refuses to be consoled over what is lost].

Thus she, in her love, for her supposed loss or taking away. And what shall become of us in ours then? That lose Him 1. not once, not oft; 2. and not in suppose as she did, but in very deed; 3. and that by sin, the worst loss of all; 4. and that not by any other's taking away, but by our own act and wilful default; and are not grieved, nay not moved a whit, break none of our wonted sports for it, as if we reckoned Him as good lost as found. Yea, when Christ and the Holy Ghost, and the favour of God, and all is gone, how soon, how easily are we comforted again for all this! that none shall need to say, *quid ploras?* to us rather, *quid non ploras?* ask us why we weep not, having so good cause to do it as we then have? This for the Angels' part.

Ver. 14. 'When she had thus said, she turned herself about, and saw Jesus standing, and knew not that it was Jesus.'

Always the Angels, we see, touched the right string, and she tells them the wrong cause, but yet the right, if it had been right.

Now to this answer of hers they would have replied, and taken away her error touching her Lord's taking away; that if she knew all, she would have left her seeking, and set her down by them, and left her weeping, and been in white as well as they.

But here is a *supersedeas* [replacement] to them, the Lord Himself comes in place. Now come we from the seeking Him dead, to the finding Him alive. For when He saw no Angels, no sight, no speech of theirs would serve, none but her Lord could give her any comfort, her Lord comes. *Christus adest.*

Adest Christus, nec ab eis unquam abest a quibus quæritur, saith Augustine; 'Christ is found, found by her; and this case of hers shall be the case of all that seriously seek Him.' This woman here for one, she sought Him we see. They that went to Emmaus to day, they but talked of Him sadly, and they both found Him.[28] Why, He is found of them that seek Him not;[29] but of them that seek Him, never but found. 'For Thou Lord never failest them that seek Thee.'[30] 'God is not unrighteous, to forget the work and labour of their love that seek Him.'[31]

So find Him they shall, but happily not all so fully at first, no more than she did. For first, to try her yet a little farther, He comes unknown, stands by her, and she little thought it had been He.

A case that likewise falls out full oft. Doubtless, 'He is not far from every one of us,' saith the Apostle to the Athenians.[32] But He is nearer us many times than we think; even hard by us and we not aware of it, saith Job.[33] And *O si cognovisses et tu*, O if we did know, and it standeth us in hand to pray that we may know when He is so, for that is 'the time of our visitation'.[34]

St John saith here, the Angels were sitting; St Luke saith, they stood.[35] They are thus reconciled. That Christ coming in presence, the Angels which before were sitting stood up. Their standing up made Mary Magdalene turn her to see who it was they rose to. And so Christ she saw, but knew Him not.

Not only not knew Him, but mis-knew Him, took Him for the

---

[28] Luke 24:13-31
[29] Isaiah 65:1
[30] Psalm 9:10
[31] Hebrews 6:10

[32] Acts 17:27
[33] Job 9:11
[34] Luke 19:42, 44
[35] Luke 24:4

gardener. Tears will dim the sight, and it was not yet scarce day, and she seeing one, and not knowing what any one should make in the ground so early but he that dressed it, she might well mistake. But it was more than so; her eyes were not holden only that she did not know Him,[36] but over and beside He did appear ἑτέρᾳ μορφῇ [in another form], in some such shape as might resemble the gardener whom she took Him for.

Proper enough it was, it fitted well the time and place, this person. The time, it was the spring; the place, it was the garden: that place is most in request at that time, for that place and time a gardener doth well.

Of which her so taking Him, St Gregory saith well, *profecto errando non erravit* [she did not err in making this error]. She did not mistake in taking Him for a gardener; though she might seem to err in some sense, yet in some other she was in the right. For in a sense, and a good sense, Christ may well be said to be a gardener, and indeed is one. For our rule is, Christ as He appears, so He is ever; no false semblant in Him.

1. A gardener He is then. The first, the fairest garden that ever was, Paradise, He was the gardener, it was of His planting. So, a gardener.

2. And ever since it is He That as God makes all our gardens green, sends us yearly the spring, and all the herbs and flowers we then gather; and neither Paul with his planting, nor Apollos with his watering, could do any good without Him.[38] So a gardener in that sense.

3. But not in that alone; but He it is that gardens our 'souls' too, and makes them, as the Prophet saith, 'like a well-watered garden'; [39] weeds out of them whatsoever is noisome or unsavory, sows and plants them with true roots and seeds of righteousness, waters them with the dew of His grace, and makes them bring forth fruit to eternal life.

But it is none of all these, but besides all these, nay over and above all these, this day if ever, most properly He was a gardener. Was one, and so after a more peculiar manner might take this

---

[36] Luke 24:16
[37] Mark 16:12

[38] 1 Corinthians 3:6
[39] Jeremiah 31:12

likeness on Him. Christ rising was indeed a gardener, and that a strange one, Who made such an herb grow out of the ground this day as the like was never seen before, a dead body to shoot forth alive out of the grave.

I ask, was He so this day alone? No, but this profession of His, this day begun, He will follow to the end. For He it is That by virtue of this morning's act shall garden our bodies too, turn all our graves into garden plots; yea, shall one day turn land and sea and all into a great garden, and so husband them as they shall in due time bring forth live bodies, even all our bodies alive again.

Long before, did Esay see this and sing of it in his song, resembling the resurrection to a spring garden. 'Awake and sing,' saith he; 'ye that dwell for a time are as it were sown in the dust, for His dew shall be as the dew of herbs, and the earth shall shoot forth her dead.'[40] So then, He appeared no other than He was; a gardener He was, not in show alone, but *opere et veritate* [in function and in truth], and so came in His own likeness. This for Christ's appearing. Now to His speech, but as unknown still.

Ver. 15. 'Jesus saith to her, Woman, why weepest thou? whom seekest thou?' She, supposing He had been the gardener, said to Him, 'Sir, if thou have borne Him hence, tell me where thou hast laid Him, and I will take Him thence.'

Still she weeps; so He begins with *Quid ploras?* asks the same questions the Angels had before; only quickens it a little with *quem quæris*, 'whom seek you?' So, *Quem quæris quærit a te, Quem quæris?* Whom she sought, He asks her 'Whom she sought'. *Si quæris, cur non cognoscis? si cognoscis, cur quæris?* saith Augustine. If she seek Him, why knows she Him not? If she know Him, why seeks she Him still? A common thing with us, this also; to seek a thing, and when we have found it, not to know we have so, but even *Christum a Christo quærere*, 'to ask Christ for Christ'. Which however it fall in other matters, in this seeking of Christ it is safe. Even when we seek Christ, to pray to Christ to help us find Christ; we shall do it full evil without Him.

This *quid ploras?* it comes now twice. The Angels asked it, we

---

40 Isaiah 26:19

stood not on it then. Now, seeing Christ asks it again the second time, we will think there is something in it, and stay a little at it. The rather, for that it is the very opening of His mouth, the very first words that ever came from Him, that He spake first of all, after His rising again from death. There is sure some more than ordinary matter in this *quid ploras?* if it be, but even for that.

Thus say the Fathers; 1. That Mary Magdalene standing by the grave's side, and there weeping, is thus brought in to represent unto us the state of all mankind before this day, the day of Christ's rising again, weeping over the dead, as do the heathen 'that have no hope';[41] comes Christ with His *quid ploras*, 'Why do you weep?' As much to say, as *ne ploras*; 'Weep not, why should you weep?' there is no cause of weeping now. Henceforth none shall need to stand by the grave to weep there any more. A question very proper for Easter-day, for the day of the Resurrection. For if there be a rising again, *quid ploras?* is right, why should she, why should any weep then?

So that this *quid ploras* of Christ's wipes away tears from all eyes, and as we sing in the thirtieth Psalm, whose title is, the Psalm of the Resurrection, puts off our 'sackcloth', that is our mourning weeds, girds us 'with gladness',[42] puts us all in white with the Angels.

Ploras then, leave that for Good-Friday, for His Passion; weep then, and spare not. But *quid ploras?* for Easter-day is in kind the feast of the Resurrection, why should there be any weeping upon it? Is not Christ risen? Shall not He raise us with Him? Is He not a gardener, to make our bodies sown to grow again? *Ploras*, leave that to the heathen that are without hope; but to the Christian man, *quid ploras?* Why should he weep? he hath hopes; the Head is already risen, the members shall in their due time follow Him.

I observe that four times this day, at four several appearings, 1. at the first, at this here, He asked her, *quid ploras?* why she wept. 2. Of them that went to Emmaus, *quid tristes estis?* Why are ye sad?[43] 3. Within a verse following, the nineteenth, He saith to the Eleven, *Pax vobis*, 'Peace be to them':[44] 4. And to the women

---

[41] 1 Thessalonians 4:13　　　　　　[43] Luke 24:17
[42] Psalm 30:11　　　　　　　　　　[44] Luke 24:36

that met Him on the way, χαίρετε, that is, rejoice, be glad.[45] So, no weeping, no being sad; now, nothing this day, but peace and joy; they do properly belong to this feast.

And this I note the more willingly now this year, because the last Easter we could not so well have noted it. Some wept then; all were sad, little joy there was, and there was a *quid*, a good cause for it.[46] But blessed be God That hath now sent us a more kindly Easter, of this, by taking away the cause of our sorrow then, that we may preach of *Quid ploras?* and be far from it. So much for *Quid ploras?* Christ's question. Now to her answer.

She is still where she was; at *sustulerunt* before, at *sustulisti* now – *si tu sustulisti*: we shall never get that word from her.

But to Christ she seems somewhat more harsh than to the Angels. To them she complains of others; 'they have taken'. Christ she seems to charge, at least to suspect of the fact, as if He looked like one that had been a breaker up of graves, a carrier away of corpses out of their place of rest. Her *if* implies as much. But pardon love; as it fears where it needs not, so it suspects oft where it hath no cause. He, or any that comes in our way, hath done it, hath taken Him away, when love is at a loss. But Bernard speaks to Christ for her; *Domine, amor quem habebat in Te, et dolor quem habebat de Te, excuset eam apud Te, si forte erravit circa Te*: that 'the love she bare to Him, the sorrow she had for Him, may excuse her with Him, if she were in any error concerning Him in her saying,' *Si tu sustulisti*.

And yet see how God shall direct the tongue! In thus charging Him, *Prophetat et nescit*, 'she says truer than she was aware.' For indeed, if any took Him away, it was He did it. So she was not much amiss. Her *si tu* was true, though not in her sense. For, *quod de Ipso factum est, Ipse fecit*, 'All that was done to Him, He did it Himself.' His taking away, *virtus fuit, non facinus*, 'was by His own power, not by the act of any other'; *et gloria, non injuria*, 'no other man's injury it was, but His own glory', that she found Him not there. This was true, but this was no part of her meaning.

---

[45] Matthew 28:9

[46] Probably referring to the death of the queen, Anne

104

I cannot here pass over two more characters of her love, that so you may have the full ten I promised.

One, in *si tu sustulisti Eum*, in her *Eum*, in her 'Him'. Him? Which Him? Her affections seem so to transport her, as she says no man knows what. To one, a mere stranger to her, and she to him, she talks of one thrice under the term of 'Him'; 'if thou hast taken Him away, tell me where thou hast laid Him, and I will fetch Him'; Him, Him, and Him, and never names Him, or tells who He is. This is *Solæcismus amoris* [Love's mistake], an irregular speech, but love's own dialect. 'Him' is enough with love: who knows not who that is? It supposes every body, all the world bound to take notice of Him Whom we look for, only by saying 'Him'; though we never tell His name, nor say a word more. *Amor, quem ipse cogitat, neminem putans ignorare* [Love considers no one ignorant of its object].

The other is in her *ego tollam*: if He would tell her where He has laid Him, she would go fetch Him, that she would. Alas poor woman, she was not able to lift Him. There are more than one, or two either, allowed to the carrying of a corpse.

As for His, it had more than a hundred pound weight of myrrh and other odours upon it,[47] beside the poise of a dead body. She could not do it. Well, yet she would do it though. *O mulier, non mulier* [O woman, not a woman], saith Origen, for *ego tollam* seems rather the speech of a porter, or of some lusty strong fellow at least, than of a silly weak woman. But love makes women more than women, at least it makes them have νοῦν ὑπὲρ ἰσχὺν, the courage above the strength, far. Never measures her own forces, no burden too heavy, no assay too hard for love, *et nihil erubescit nisi nomen difficultatis*, 'and is not ashamed of any thing, but that any thing should be too hard or too heavy for it.' *Affectus sine mensurâ virium propriarum* [Inspired without reference to normal strength]. Both these argue *dilexit multum* [she loved much]. And so now, you have the full number of ten.

Ver. 16. 'Jesus saith to her, Mary; she turned herself, and said to Him, Rabboni, that is to say, Master.'

---

[47] John 19:39

Now *magnes amoris amor*; 'nothing so allures, so draws love to it, as doth love itself.' In Christ specially, and in such in whom the same mind is. For when her Lord saw there was no taking away His taking away from her, all was in vain, neither men, nor Angels, nor Himself, so long as He kept Himself gardener, could get any thing of her but her Lord was gone, He was taken away, and that for the want of Jesus nothing but Jesus could yield her any comfort, He is no longer able to contain, but even discloses Himself; and discloses Himself by His voice.

For it should seem before, with His shape He had changed that also. But now He speaks to her in His known voice, in the wonted accent of it, does but name her name, Mary – no more, and that was enough. That was as much to say, *Recognosce a quo recognosceris*, 'she would at least take notice of Him, that shewed He was no stranger by calling her by her name'; for whom we call by their names, we take particular notice of. So God says to Moses, *Te autem cognovi de nomine*, 'thou hast found grace in My sight, and I know thee by name.'[48] As God Moses, so Christ Mary Magdalene.

And this indeed is the right way to know Christ, to be known of Him first. The Apostle saith, now we 'have known God', and then correcteth himself, 'or rather have been known of God.'[49] For till He know us, we shall never know Him aright.

And now, lo Christ is found; found alive, That was sought dead. A cloud may be so thick we shall not see the sun through it. The sun must scatter that cloud, and then we may. Here is an example of it. It is strange a thick cloud of heaviness had so covered her, as see Him she could not through it; this one word, these two syllables, Mary, from His mouth, scatters it all. No sooner had His voice sounded in her ears but it drives away all the mist, dries up her tears, lightens her eyes, that she knew Him straight, and answers Him with her wonted salutation, 'Rabboni.' If it had lain in her power to have raised Him from the dead, she would not have failed but done it, I dare say. Now it is done to her hands.

---

[48] Exodus 33:17   [49] Galatians 4:9

And with this all is turned out and in; a new world now. Away with *sustulerunt*; His taking away, is taken away quite. For if His taking away were her sorrow, *contrariorum contraria consequentia* [the opposite is consequently the opposite]. *Si de sublato ploravit, de suscitato exultavit*, we may be sure; 'if sad for His death, for His taking away, then glad for His rising, for His restoring again.' Surely if she would have been glad but to have found but His dead body, now she finds it and Him alive, what was her joy, how great may we think! So that by this she saw *Quid ploras* was not asked her for nought, that it was no impertinent question, as it fell out. Well now, He that was thought lost is found again, and found, not as He was sought for, not a dead body, but 'a living soul'; nay, 'a quickening Spirit' then.[50] And that might Mary Magdalene well say. He shewed it, for He quickened her, and her spirits that were as good as dead. You thought you should have come to Christ's resurrection to-day, and so you do. But not to His alone, but even to Mary Magdalene's resurrection too. For in very deed a kind of resurrection it was was wrought in her; revived as it were, and raised from a dead and drooping, to a lively and cheerful estate. The gardener had done His part, made her all green on the sudden.

And all this by a word of His mouth. Such power is there in every word of His; so easily are they called, whom Christ will but speak to.

But by this we see, when He would be made known to her after His rising, He did choose to be made known by the ear rather than by the eye. By hearing rather than by appearing. Opens her ears first, and her eyes after. Her 'eyes were holden'[51] till her ears were opened; comes *aures autem aperuisti mihi* [mine ears hast thou opened],[52] and that opens them.

With the philosophers, hearing is the sense of wisdom. With us, in divinity, it is the sense of faith. So, most meet. Christ is the word; hearing then, that sense, is Christ's sense; *voce quam visu* [by voice rather than by sight], more proper to the word. So, *sicut audivimus* [as we have heard] goes before, and then *sic vidimus*

---

[50] 1 Corinthians 15:45   [52] Psalm 40:6
[51] Luke 24:16

107

[as we have seen] comes after.[53] In matters of faith the ear goes first ever, and is of more use, and to be trusted before the eye. For in many cases faith holdeth, where sight faileth.

This then is a good way to come to the knowledge of Christ, by *hodie si vocem*, to 'hear His voice'.[54] Howbeit, it is not the only way. There is another way to take notice of Him by besides, and we to take notice of it. On this very day we have them both.

For twice this day came Christ; unknown first, and then known after. To Mary Magdalene here, and to them at Emmaus. To Mary Magdalene unknown, in the shape of a gardener. To those that went to Emmaus unknown, in the likeness of a traveller by the way-side. Come to be known to her by His voice, by the word of His mouth. Not so to them. For many words He spake to them, and they felt them warm at their hearts, but knew Him not for all that. But 'He was known to them in the breaking of the bread.'[55] Her eyes opened by speaking a word; their eyes opened by the breaking of bread. There is the one and the other way, and so now you have both. And now you have them, I pray you make use of them. I see I shall not be able to go farther than this verse.

It were a folly to fall to comparisons, *committere inter se*, to set them at odds together these two ways, as the fond fashion now-a-days is, whether is better, Prayer or Preaching; the Word or the Sacraments. What needs this? Seeing we have both, both are ready for us; the one now, the other by-and-by; we may end this question soon. And this is the best and surest way to end it; to esteem of them both, to thank Him for both, to make use of both; having now done with one, to make trial of the other. It may be, who knows? if the one will not work, the other may. And if by the one or by the other, by either if it be wrought, what harm have we? In case it be not, yet have we offered to God our service in both, and committed the success of both to Him. He will see they shall have success, and in His good time, as shall be expedient for us, vouchsafe every one of us as He did Mary Magdalene in the text, 'to know Him and the virtue of His resurrection';[56] and

---

[53]Psalm 48:8
[54] Psalm 95:7
[55] Luke 24:30-35
[56] Philippians 3:10

make us partakers of both, by both the means before remembered, by His blessed word, by His holy mysteries; the means to
raise our souls here, the pledges of the raising up of our bodies
hereafter. Of both which He makes us partakers,[57] Who is the
Author of both, 'Jesus Christ the Righteous', &c.

---

[57] 1 John 2:1

A Sermon

PREACHED BEFORE THE

KING'S MAJESTY, AT WHITEHALL

on Wednesday, the Twenty-Fifth of December, A.D. MDCXXII.
Being Christmas-Day.

Matthew ii: 1, 2.

Behold there came wise men from the East to Jerusalem,
Saying, Where is the King of the Jews That is born? For we have seen
His star in the East, and are come to worship Him.

[*Ecce magi ab Oriente venerunt Jerosolymam,*
Dicentes, Ubi est Qui natus est Rex Judæorum? vidimus enim
stellam Ejus in Oriente, et venimus adorare Eum.   Latin Vulg.]

[*Behold, there came wise men from the East to Jerusalem,*
Saying, Where is He That is born King of the Jews? for we have seen
His star in the East, and are come to worship Him.
Authorized Version]

.

There be in these two verses two principal points, as was observed
when time was; 1. The persons that arrived at Jerusalem, 2. and
their errand. The persons in the former verse, whereof hath been
treated heretofore. Their errand in the latter, whereof we are
now to deal.

Their errand we may best learn from themselves out of their
dicentes, &c. Which, in a word, is to worship Him. Their errand
our errand, and the errand of this day.

This text may seem to come a little too soon, before the time;
and should have stayed till the day it was spoken on, rather than
on this day. But if you mark them well, there are in the verse four
words that be *verba diei hujus*, 'proper and peculiar to this very
day'. 1. For first, *natus est* is most proper to this day of all days,
the day of His Nativity. 2. Secondly, *vidimus stellam*; for on this
day it was first seen, appeared first. 3. Thirdly, *venimus*; for this
day they set forth, began their journey. 4. And last, *adorare Eum*;
for 'when He brought His only-begotten Son into the world, He

110

gave in charge, Let all the Angels of God worship Him.'[1] And when the Angels to do it, no time more proper for us to do it as then. So these four appropriate it to this day, and none but this.

The main heads of their errand are 1. *Vidimus stellam*, the occasion; 2. and *Venimus adorare*, the end of their coming. But for the better conceiving it I will take another course, to set forth these points to be handled.

Their faith first: faith – in that they never ask 'Whether He be', but 'Where He is born'; for that born He is, that they stedfastly believe.

Then 'the work or service' of this faith, as St Paul calleth it; 'the touch or trial', δοκίμιον, as St Peter; the *ostende mihi* [show me], as St James;[2] of this their faith in these five. 1. Their confessing of it in *venerunt dicentes*. *Venerunt*, they were no sooner come, but *dicentes*, they tell it out; confess Him and His birth to be the cause of their coming. 2. Secondly, as confess their faith, so the ground of their faith; *vidimus enim*, for they had 'seen' His star; and His star being risen, by it they knew He must be risen too. 3. Thirdly, as St Paul calls them in Abraham's, *vestigia fidei*, 'the steps of their faith',[3] in *venimus*, 'their coming' – coming such a journey, at such a time, with such speed. 4. Fourthly, when they were come, their diligent enquiring Him out by *ubi est?* for here is the place of it, asking after Him to find where He was. 5. And last, when they had found Him, the end of their seeing, coming, seeking; and all for no other end but to worship Him. Here they say it, at the 11th verse they do it in these two acts; 1. *procidentes*, their 'falling down', 2. and *obtulerunt*, their 'offering' to Him. Worship Him with their bodies, worship Him with their goods; their worship and ours the true worship of Christ.

The text is of a star, and we may make all run on a star, that so the text and day may be suitable, and Heaven and earth hold a correspondence. St Peter calls faith 'the day-star rising in our hearts',[4] which sorts well with the star in the text rising in the sky. That in the sky manifesting itself from above to them; this

---

[1] Hebrews 1:6
[2] Philippians 2:17; 1 Peter 1:7
James 2:18

[3] Romans 4:12
[4] 2 Peter 1:19

111

in their hearts manifesting itself from below to Him, to Christ. Manifesting itself by these five: 1. by *ore fit confessio*, 'the confessing of it'; 2. by *fides est substantia*, 'the ground of it'; 3. by *vestigia fidei*, 'the steps of it'[5] in their painful coming; 4. by their *ubi est?* 'careful enquiring'; 5. and last, by *adorare Eum*, 'their devout worshipping'. These five, as so many beams of faith, the day-star risen in their hearts. To take notice of them. For every one of them is of the nature óf a condition, so as if we fail in them, *non lucet nobis stella hæc*, 'we have no part in the light, or conduct of this star.' Neither in *stellam*, 'the star itself', nor in *Ejus*, 'in Him Whose the star is'; that is, not in Christ neither.

We have now got us a star on earth for that in Heaven, and these both lead us to a third. So as upon the matter three stars we have, and each his proper manifestation. 1. The first in the firmament; that appeared unto them, and in them to us – a figure of St Paul's Ἐπεφάνη χάρις, 'the grace of God appearing and bringing salvation to all men',[6] Jews and Gentiles all. 2. The second here on earth is St Peter's *Lucifer in cordibus* [day star in your hearts];[7] and this appeared in them, and so must in us. Appeared 1. in their eyes – *vidimus*; 2. in their feet – *venimus*; 3. in their lips – *dicentes ubi est*; 4. in their knees – *procidentes*, 'falling down'; 5. in their hands – *obtulerunt*, 'by offering'. These five every one a beam of this star. 3. The third in Christ Himself, St John's star. 'The generation and root of David, the bright morning Star, Christ.'[8] And He, His double appearing. 1. One at this time now, when He appeared in great humility; and we see and come to Him by faith. 2. The other, which we wait for, even 'the blessed hope, and appearing of the great God and our Saviour'[9] in the majesty of His glory.

These three: 1. The first that manifested Christ to them; 2. The second that manifested them to Christ; 3. The third Christ Himself, in Whom both these were as it were in conjunction. Christ 'the bright morning Star' of that day which shall have no night; the *beatifica visio*, 'the blessed sight' of which day is the *consummatum est* [it is finished] of our hope and happiness for ever.

---

[5] Romans 10:10; Hebrews 11:1;
   Romans 4:12
[6] Titus 2:11
[7] 2 Peter 1:19
[8] Revelation 22:16
[9] Titus 2:13

Of these three stars the first is gone, the third yet to come, the second only is present. We to look to that, and to the five beams of it. That is it must do us all the good, and bring us to the third.

St Luke calleth faith the 'door of faith'.[10] At this door let us enter. Here is a coming, and 'he that cometh to God', and so he that to Christ, 'must believe, that Christ is':[11] so do these. They never ask *an sit*, but *ubi sit*? Not 'whether', but 'where He is born'. They that ask *ubi Qui natus*? take *natus* for granted, presuppose that born He is. Herein is faith – faith of Christ's being born, the third article of the Christian Creed.

And what believe they of Him? Out of their own words here; 1. first that *natus*, that 'born' He is, and so Man He is – His human nature. 1. And as His nature, so His office in *natus est Rex*, 'born a King'. They believe that too. 3. But *Judæorum* may seem to be a bar; for then, what have they to do with 'the King of the Jews'? They be Gentiles, none of His lieges, no relation to Him at all: what do they seeking or worshipping Him? But weigh it well, and it is no bar. For this they seem to believe: He is so *Rex Judæorum*, 'King of the Jews', as He is *adorandus a Gentibus*, 'the Gentiles to adore Him'. And though born in Jewry, yet Whose birth concerned them though Gentiles, though born far off in the 'mountains of the East'. They to have some benefit by Him and His birth, and for that to do Him worship, seeing *officium fundator in beneficio* [worship is founded in benefit] ever. 4. As thus born in earth, so a star He hath in Heaven of His own – *stellam Ejus*, 'His star'; He the owner of it. Now we know the stars are the stars of Heaven, and He that Lord of them Lord of Heaven too; and so to be adored of them, of us, and of all. St John puts them together; 'the root and generation of David', His earthly; and 'the bright morning star',[12] His Heavenly or Divine generation. *Hæc est fides Magorum*, this is the mystery of their faith. In *natus est*, man; in *stellam Ejus*, God. In *Rex*, 'a King', though of the Jews, yet the good of Whose Kingdom should extend and stretch itself far and wide to Gentiles and all; and He of all to be adored. This, for *corde creditur* [to believe in the heart], the day-star itself in their hearts.[13] Now to the beams of this star.

---

[10] Acts 14:27
[11] Hebrews 11:6
[12] Revelation 22:16
[13] 2 Peter 1:19

Next to *corde creditur* is *ore fit confessio*, 'the confession' of this faith. It is in *venerunt dicentes*, they came with it in their mouths. *Venerunt*, they were no sooner come, but they spake of it so freely, to so many, as it came to Herod's ear and troubled him not a little that any King of the Jews should be worshipped beside himself. So then their faith is no bosom-faith, kept to themselves without ever a *dicentes*, without saying any thing of it to any body. No; *credidi, propter quod locutus sum*, 'they believed, and therefore they spake.'[14] The star in their hearts cast one beam out at their mouths. And though Herod who was but *Rex factus* [a puppet king] could evil brook to hear of *Rex natus* [a born king], – must needs be offended at it, yet they were not afraid to say it. And though they came from the East, those parts to whom and their King the Jews had long time been captives and their underlings, they were not ashamed neither to tell, that One of the Jews' race they came to seek; and to seek Him to the end 'to worship Him'. So neither afraid of Herod, nor ashamed of Christ; but professed their errand, and cared not who knew it. This for their confessing Him boldly.

But faith is said by the Apostle to be ὑπόστασις [substance], and so there is a good 'ground'; and ἔλεγχος [evidence], and so hath a good 'reason' for it.[15] This puts the difference between *fidelis* and *credulus*, or as Solomon terms him *fatuus, qui credit omni verbo* [the simple, who believe every word];[16] between faith and lightness of belief. Faith hath ever a ground; *vidimus enim*, – an *enim*, a reason for it, and is ready to render it. How came you to believe? *Audivimus enim*, 'for we have heard an Angel,' say the shepherds.[17] *Vidimus enim*, 'for we have seen a star' say the Magi, and this is a well-grounded faith. We came not of our own heads, we came not before we saw some reason for it – saw that which set us on coming; *Vidimus enim stellam Ejus*.

Vidimus stellam – we can well conceive that; any that will but look up, may see a star. But how could they see the *Ejus* of it, that it was His? Either that it belonged to any, or that He it was it belonged to. This passeth all perspective; no astronomy could

---

14 Psalm 116:10
15 Hebrews 11:1

16 Proverbs 14:15
17 Luke 2:20

114

shew them this. What by course of nature the stars can produce, that they by course of art or observation may discover. But this birth was above nature. No trigon, triplicity, exaltation could bring it forth. They are but idle that set figures for it. The star should not have been His, but He the star's, if it had gone that way. Some other light then, they saw this *Ejus* by.

Now with us in Divinity there be but two in all; 1. *Vespertina*, and 2. *Matutina lux. Vespertina*, 'the owl-light' of our reason or skill is too dim to see it by. No remedy then but it must be as Esay calls it, *matutina lux*, 'the morning-light',[18] the light of God's law must certify them of the *Ejus* of it. There, or not at all to be had whom this star did portend.

And in the Law, there we find it in the twenty-fourth of Numbers.[19] One of their own Prophets that came from whence they came, 'from the mountains of the East', was ravished in spirit, 'fell in a trance, had his eyes opened', and saw the *Ejus* of it many an hundred years before it rose. Saw *orietur in Jacob* [there shall come (a star) out of Jacob], that there it should 'rise', which is as much as *natus est* here. Saw *stella*, that He should be 'the bright morning-Star', and so might well have a star to represent Him. Saw *sceptrum in Israel* [a Sceptre out of Israel], which is just as much as *Rex Judæorum*, that it should portend a King there – such a King as should not only 'smite the corners of Moab', that is Balak their enemy for the present; but 'should reduce and bring under Him all the sons of Seth', that is all the world; for all are now Seth's sons, Cain's were all drowned in the flood. Here now is the *Ejus* of it clear. A Prophet's eye might discern this; never a Chaldean of them all could take it with his astrolabe. Balaam's eyes were opened to see it, and he helped to open their eyes by leaving behind him this prophecy to direct them how to apply it, when it should arise to the right *Ejus* of it.

But these had not the law. It is hard to say that the Chaldee paraphrase was extant long before this. They might have had it. Say, they had it not: if Moses were so careful to record this prophecy in his book, it may well be thought that some memory

---

18 Isaiah 58:8   19 Numbers 24:16-17

115

of this so memorable a prediction was left remaining among them of the East, his own country where he was born and brought up. And some help they might have from Daniel too, who lived all his time in Chaldea and Persia, and prophesied among them of such a King, and set the just time of it.

And this, as it is conceived, put the difference between the East and the West. For I ask, was it *vidimus in Oriente* with them? Was it not *vidimus in Occidente* [we have seen in the West]? In the West such a star – it or the fellow of it was seen nigh about that time, or the Roman stories deceive us. Toward the end of Augustus' reign such a star was seen, and much scanning there was about it. Pliny saith it was generally holden, that star to be *faustum sydus*, 'a lucky comet', and portended good to the world, which few or no comets do.[20] And Virgil, who then lived, would needs take upon him to set down the *ejus* of it, ... *Ecce Dionæi*, &c. – entitled Cæsar to it. And verily there is no man that can without admiration read his sixth Eclogue, of a birth that time expected, that should be the offspring of the gods, and that should take away their sins.[21] Whereupon it hath gone for current – the East and West, *Vidimus* both.

But by the light of their prophecy, the East they went straight to the right *Ejus*. And for want of this light the West wandered, and gave it a wrong *ejus*; as Virgil, applying it to little Salonine: and as evil hap was, while he was making his verses, the poor child died; and so his star shot, vanished, and came to nothing. Their *vidimus* never came to a *venimus*; they neither went, nor worshipped Him as these here did.

But by this we see, when all is done, hither we must come for our morning-light; to this book, to the word of prophecy. All our *vidimus stellam* is as good as nothing without it. That star is past and gone, long since; 'Heaven and earth shall pass, but this word shall not pass.'[22] Here on this, we to fix our eye and to ground our faith. Having this, though we neither hear Angel nor see star, we may by the grace of God do full well. For even they that have had

---

[20] Pliny, *Natural History*, II.xxiii

[21] Virgil, *Eclogues*, IX.47; IV.48-9 (Andrewes has made a mistake here)

[22] Luke 21:33

both those, have been fain to resolve into this as their last, best, and chiefest point of all. Witness St Peter: he, saith he, and they with him, 'saw Christ's glory, and heard the voice from Heaven in the Holy Mount.'[23] What then? After both these, *audivimus* and *vidimus*, both senses, he comes to this, *Habemus autem firmiorem, &c.* 'We have a more sure word of prophecy' than both these; *firmiorem*, a 'more sure', a more clear, than them both. And *si hîc legimus* – for *legimus* is *vidimus*, 'if here we read it written', it is enough to ground our faith, and let the star go.

And yet, to end this point; both these, the star and the prophecy, they are but *circumfusa lux* [a light poured around us] – without both. Besides these there must be a light within in the eye; else, we know, for all them nothing will be seen. And that must come from Him, and the enlightening of His Spirit. Take this for a rule; no knowing of *Ejus absque Eo*, 'of His without Him', Whose it is. Neither of the star, without Him That created it; nor of the prophecy, without Him That inspired it. But this third coming too; He sending the light of His Spirit within into their minds, they then saw clearly, this the star, now the time, He the Child That this day was born.

He That sent these two without, sent also this third within, and then it was *vidimus* indeed. The light of the star in their eyes, the 'word of prophecy' in their ears, the beam of His Spirit in their hearts; these three made up a full *vidimus*. And so much for *vidimus stellam Ejus*, the occasion of their coming.

Now to *venimus*, their coming itself. And it follows well. For it is not a star only, but a load-star; and whither should *stella Ejus ducere*, but *ad Eum*? 'Whither lead us, but to Him Whose the star is?' The star to the star's Master.

All this while we have been at *dicentes*, 'saying' and seeing; now we shall come to *facientes*, see them do somewhat upon it. It is not saying nor seeing will serve St James; he will call, and be still calling for *ostende mihi*, 'shew my thy faith by some work.'[24] And well may he be allowed to call for it this day; it is the day of *vidimus*, appearing, being seen. You have seen His star, let Him

---

[23] 2 Peter 1:16-19   [24] James 2:18

now see your star another while. And so they do. Make your faith to be seen; so it is – their faith in the steps of their faith. And so was Abraham's first by coming forth of his country; as these here do, and so 'walk in the steps of the faith of Abraham',[25] do his first work.

It is not commended to stand 'gazing up into Heaven' too long;[26] not on Christ Himself ascending, much less on His star. For they sat not still gazing on the star. Their *vidimus* begat *venimus*; their seeing made them come, come a great journey. *Venimus* is soon said, but a short word; but many a wide and weary step they made before they could come to say *Venimus*, Lo, here 'we are come'; come, and at our journey's end. To look a little on it. In this their coming we consider, 1. First, the distance of the place they came from. It was not hard by as the shepherds – but a step to Bethlehem over the fields; this was riding many a hundred miles, and cost them many a day's journey. 2. Secondly, we consider the way that they came, if it be pleasant, or plain and easy; for if it be, it is so much the better. 1. This was nothing pleasant, for through deserts, all the way waste and desolate. 2. Nor secondly, easy neither; for over the rocks and crags of both Arabias, specially Petræa, their journey lay. 3. Yet if safe – but it was not, but exceeding dangerous, as lying through the midst of the 'black tents of Kedar',[27] a nation of thieves and cut-throats; to pass over the hills of robbers, infamous then, and infamous to this day. No passing without great troop or convoy. 4. Last we consider the time of their coming, the season of the year. It was no summer progress. A cold coming they had of it at this time of the year, just the worst time of the year to take a journey, and specially a long journey in. The ways deep, the weather sharp, the days short, the sun farthest off, in *solstitio brumali*, 'the very dead of winter'. *Venimus*, 'we are come', if that be one, *venimus*, 'we are now come', come at this time, that sure is another.

And these difficulties they overcame, of a wearisome, irksome, troublesome, dangerous, unseasonable journey; and for all this they came. And came it cheerfully and quickly, as appeareth by

---

[25] Romans 4:12
[26] Acts 1:11

[27] Song of Solomon 1:4

the speed they made. It was but *vidimus, venimus*, with them; 'they saw', and 'they came'; no sooner saw, but they set out presently. So as upon the first appearing of the star, as it might be last night, they knew it was Balaam's star; it called them away, they made ready straight to begin their journey this morning. A sign they were highly conceited of His birth, believed some great matter of it, that they took all these pains, made all this haste that they might be there to worship Him with all the possible speed they could. Sorry for nothing so much as that they could not be there soon enough, with the very first, to do it even this day, the day of His birth. All considered, there is more in *venimus* than shews at the first sight. It was not for nothing it was said in the first verse, *ecce venerunt*; their coming hath an *ecce* on it, it well deserves it.

And we, what should we have done? Sure these men of the East shall rise in judgment against the men of the West, that is us, and their faith against ours in this point. With them it was but *vidimus, venimus*; with us it would have been but *veniemus* [we will come] at most. Our fashion is to see and see again before we stir a foot, specially if it be to the worship of Christ. Come such a journey at such a time? No; but fairly have put it off to the spring of the year, till the days longer, and the ways fairer, and the weather warmer, till better travelling to Christ. Our Epiphany would sure have fallen in Easter-week at the soonest.

But then for the distance, desolateness, tediousness, and the rest, any of them were enough to mar our *venimus* quite. It must be no great way, first, we must come; we love not that. Well fare the shepherds, yet they came but hard by; rather like them than the Magi. Nay, not like them neither. For with us the nearer, lightly the farther off; our proverb is you know, 'The nearer the Church, the farther from God.'

Nor it must not be through no desert, over no Petræa. If rugged or uneven the way, if the weather ill-disposed, if any never so little danger, it is enough to stay us. To Christ we cannot travel, but weather and way and all must be fair. If not, no journey, but sit still and see farther. As indeed, all our religion is rather *vidimus*, a contemplation, than *venimus*, a motion, or stirring to do ought.

119

But when we do it, we must be allowed leisure. Ever *veniemus*, never *venimus*; ever coming, never come. We love to make no very great haste. To other things perhaps; not to *adorare*, the place of the worship of God. Why should we? Christ is no wild-cat. What talk ye of twelve days? And if it be forty days hence, ye shall be sure to find His Mother and Him; she cannot be churched till then. What needs such haste? The truth is, we conceit Him and His birth but slenderly, and our haste is even thereafter. But if we be at that point, we must be out of this *venimus*; they like enough to leave us behind. Best get us a new Christmas in September; we are not like to come to Christ at this feast. Enough for *venimus*.

But what is *venimus* without *invenimus* [we have found]? And when they come, they hit not on Him at first. No more must we think, as soon as ever we be come, to find him straight. They are fain to come to their *ubi est?* We must now look back to that. For though it stand before in the verse, here is the right place of it. They saw before they came, and came before they asked; asked before they found, and found before they worshipped. Between *venimus*, 'their coming', and *adorare*, 'their worshipping', there is the true place of *dicentes, ubi est?*

Where, first, we note a double use of their *dicentes*, these wise man had. 1. As to manifest what they knew, *natus est*, 'that He is born', so to confess and ask what they knew not, the place where. We to have the like.

2. Secondly, set down this; that to find where He is, we must learn of these to ask where He is, which we full little set ourselves to do. If we stumble on Him, so it is; but for any asking we trouble not ourselves, but sit still as we say, and let nature work; and so let grace too, and so for us it shall. I wot well, it is said in a place of Esay, 'He was found', *a non quærentibus*, 'of some that sought Him not',[28] never asked *ubi est?* But it is no good holding by that place. It was their good hap that so did. But trust not to it, it is not every body's case, that. It is better advice you shall read in the Psalm, *hæc est generatio quærentium*, 'there is a generation of them

---

[28] Isaiah 65:1

120

that seek Him.'[29] Of which these were, and of that generation let us be. Regularly there is no promise of *invenietis* but to *quærite*, of finding but to such as 'seek'. It is not safe to presume to find Him otherwise.

I thought there had been small use now of *ubi est?* Yet there is except we hold the ubiquity, that Christ is *ubi non*, 'any where'. But He is not so. Christ hath His *ubi*, His proper place where He is to be found; and if you miss of that, you miss of Him. And well may we miss, saith Christ Himself, there are so many will take upon them to tell us where, and tell us of so many *ubis. Ecce hîc*, 'Look you, here He is'; *Ecce illîc*, nay then, 'there'. *In deserto*, 'in the desert'. Nay, *in penetralibus*, 'in such a privy conventicle' you shall be sure of Him.[30] And yet He, saith He Himself, in none of them all. There is then yet place for *ubi est?* I speak not of His natural body, but of His mystical – that is Christ too.

How shall we then do? Where shall we get this 'where' resolved? Where these did. They said it to many, and oft, but gat no answer, till they had got together a convocation of Scribes, and they resolved them of Christ's *ubi*. For they in the East were nothing so wise, or well seen, as we in the West are now grown. We need call no Scribes together, and get them tell us, 'where.' Every artisan hath a whole Synod of Scribes in his brain, and can tell where Christ is better than any learned man of them all. Yet these were wise men; best learn where they did.

And how did the Scribes resolve it them? Out of Micah.[31] As before to the star they join Balaam's prophecy, so now again to His *orietur*, that such a one should be born, they had put Micah's *et tu Bethlehem* [And thou, Bethlehem], the place of His birth. Still helping, and giving light as it were to the light of Heaven, by a more clear light, the light of the Sanctuary.

Thus then to do. And to do it ourselves, and not seek Christ *per alium*; set others about it as Herod did these, and sit still ourselves. For so, we may hap never find Him no more than he did.

And now we have found 'where', what then? it is neither in seeking nor finding, *venimus* nor *invenimus*: the end of all, the

---

[29] Psalm 24:6   [31] Micah 5:2
[30] Matthew 24:23, 26

cause of all is in the last words, *adorare Eum*, 'to worship Him'. That is all in all, and without it all our seeing, coming, seeking, and finding is to no purpose. The Scribes they could tell, and did tell where He was, but were never the nearer for it, for they worshipped Him not. For this end to seek Him.

This is acknowledged: Herod, in effect, said as much. He would know where He were fain, and if they will bring him word where, he will come too and worship Him, that he will. None of that worship. If he find Him, his worshipping will prove worrying; as did appear by a sort of silly poor lambs that he worried, when he could not have his will on Christ.[32] Thus he at His birth.

And at His death, the other Herod, he sought Him too; but it was that he and his soldiers might make themselves sport with Him. Such seeking there is otherwhile. And such worshipping; as they in the judgment-hall worshipped Him with *Ave Rex* [Hail, King (of the Jews)], and then gave Him a bob blindfold.[33] The world's worship of Him for the most part.

But we may be bold to say, Herod was 'a fox'.[34] These mean as they say; to worship Him they come, and worship Him they will. Will they so? Be they well advised what they promise, before they know whether they shall find Him in a worshipful taking or no? For full little know they, where and in what case they shall find Him. What, if in a stable, laid there in a manger, and the rest suitable to it; in as poor and pitiful a plight as ever was any, more like to be abhorred than adored of such persons? Will they be as good as their word, trow? Will they not step back at the sight, repent themselves of their journey, and wish themselves at home again? But so find Him, and so finding Him, worship Him for all that? If they will, verily then great is their faith. This, the clearest beam of all.

'The Queen of the South', who was a figure of these Kings of the East, she came as great a journey as these.[35] But when she came, she found a King indeed, King Solomon in all his royalty. Saw a glorious King, and a glorious court about him. Saw him, and heard him; tried him with many hard questions, received

[32] Matthew 2:16
[33] Luke 23:11; John 19:2-3
[34] Luke 13:32
[35] Matthew 12:42

satisfaction of them all. This was worth her coming. Weigh what she found, and what these here – as poor and unlikely a birth as could be, ever to prove a King, or any great matter. No sight to comfort them, nor a word for which they any whit the wiser; nothing worth their travel. Weigh these together, and great odds will be found between her faith and theirs. Theirs the greater far.

Well, they will take Him as they find Him, and all this notwithstanding, worship Him for all that. The Star shall make amends for the manger, and for *stella Ejus* they will dispense with *Eum*.

And what is it to worship? Some great matter sure it is, that Heaven and earth, the stars and Prophets, thus do but serve to lead them and conduct us to. For all we see ends in *adorare*. *Scriptura et mundus ad hoc sunt, ut colatur Qui creavit, et adoretur Qui inspiravit*; 'the Scripture and world are but to this end, that He That created the one and inspired the other might be but worshipped.' Such reckoning did these seem to make of it here. And such the great treasurer of the Queen Candace.[36] These came from the mountains in the East; he from the uttermost part of Æthiopia came, and came for no other end but only this – to worship; and when they had done that, home again. *Tanti est adorare*. Worth the while, worth our coming, if coming we do but that, but worship and nothing else. And so I would have men account of it.

To tell you what it is in particular, I must put you over to the eleventh verse,[37] where it is set down what they did when they worshipped. It is set down in two acts προσκυνεῖν, and προσφέρειν, 'falling down', and 'offering'. Thus did they, thus we do; we to do the like when we will worship. These two are all, and more than these we find not.

We can worship God but three ways, we have but three things to worship Him withal. 1. The soul He hath inspired; 2. the body He hath ordained us; 3. and the worldly goods He hath vouchsafed to bless us withal. We to worship Him with all, seeing there is but one reason for all.

If He breathed into us our soul, but framed not our body, but

[36] Acts 8:27   [37] Matthew 2:11

some other did that, neither bow your knee nor uncover your head, but keep on your hats, and sit even as you do hardly. But if He hath framed that body of yours and every member of it, let Him have the honour both of head and knee, and every member else.

Again, if it be not He That gave us our worldly goods but somebody else, what He gave not, that withhold from Him and spare not. But if all come from Him, all to return to Him. If He send all, to be worshipped with all. And this in good sooth is but *rationabile obsequium* [reasonable service], as the Apostle calleth it.[38] No more than reason would, we should worship Him with all.

Else if all our worship be inward only, with our hearts and not our hats as some fondly imagine, we give Him but one of three; we put Him to His thirds, bid Him be content with that, He gets no more but inward worship. That is out of the text quite. For though I doubt not but these here performed that also, yet here it is not. St Matthew mentions it not, it is not to be seen, no *vidimus* on it. And the text is a *vidimus*, and of a star; that is, of an outward visible worship to be seen of all. There is a *vidimus* upon the worship of the body, it may be seen – *procidentes*. Let us see you fall down. So is there upon the worship with our worldly goods, that may be seen and felt – *offerentes*. Let us see whether, and what you offer. With both which, no less than with the soul, God is to be worshipped. 'Glorify God with your bodies, for they are God's,' saith the Apostle.[39] 'Honour God with your substance, for He hath blessed your store,' saith Solomon.[40] It is the precept of a wise King, of one there; it is the practice of more than one, of these three here. Specially now; for Christ hath now a body, for which to do Him worship with our bodies. And now He was made poor to make us rich, and so *offerentes* will do well, comes very fit.

To enter farther into these two would be too long, and indeed they be not in our verse here, and so for some other treatise at some other time.

There now remains nothing but to include ourselves, and bear

---

[38] Romans 12:1   [40] Proverbs 3:9
[39] 1 Corinthians 6:20

our part with them, and with the Angels, and all who this day adored Him.

This was the load-star of the Magi, and what were they? Gentiles. So are we. But if it must be ours, then we are to go with them; *vade, et fac similiter,* 'go, and do likewise.'[41] It is *Stella gentium*, but *idem agentium* 'the Gentiles' star', but 'such Gentiles as overtake these and keep company with them.' In their *dicentes*, 'confessing their faith freely'; in their *vidimus*, 'grounding it throughly'; in their *venimus*, 'hasting to come to Him speedily'; in their *ubi est?* 'enquiring Him out diligently'; and in their *adorare Eum*, 'worshipping Him devoutly'. *Per omnia* [in all things] doing as these did; worshipping and thus worshipping, celebrating and thus celebrating the feast of His birth.

We cannot say *vidimus stellam*; the star is gone long since, not now to be seen. Yet I hope for all that, that *venimus adorare*, 'we be come thither to worship.' It will be the more acceptable, if not seeing it we worship though. It is enough we read of it in the text; we see it there. And indeed as I said, it skills not for the star in the firmament, if the same Day-Star be risen in our hearts that was in theirs, and the same beams of it to be seen, all five. For then we have our part in it no less, nay full out as much as they. And it will bring us whither it brought them, to Christ. Who at His second appearing in glory shall call forth these wise men, and all that have ensued the steps of their faith, and that upon the reason specified in the text; for I have seen their star shining and shewing forth itself by the like beams; and as they came to worship Me, so am I come to do them worship. A *venite* then, for a *venimus* now. Their star I have seen, and give them a place above among the stars. They fell down: I will lift them up, and exalt them. And as they offered to Me, so am I come to bestow on them, and to reward them with the endless joy and bliss of My Heavenly Kingdom.

To which, &c.

---

[41] Luke 10:37

From the First Sermon of the Nativity, Christmas Day, 1605

Hebrews ii: 16.

For He in no wise took the Angels; but the seed of Abraham He took.

[*Nusquam enim Angelos apprehendit; sed semen Abrahæ apprehendit.*   Latin Vulg.]

[*For verily He took not on Him the nature of Angels; but He took on Him the seed of Abraham.*   Authorized Version]

1. Of *apprehendit* [he took], first. Many words were more obvious, and offered themselves to the Apostle, no doubt; *suscepit* [he took up], or *assumpsit* [he assumed], or other such like. 'This word was sought for, certainly, and made choice of,' saith the Greek Scholiast; and he can best tell us it is no common word, and tell us also what it weigheth; Δηλοῖ δὲ, saith he, ὅτι ἡμεῖς ἐφεύγο-μεν, ὁ δὲ ἐδίωκε, καὶ διώκων ἔφθασε, καὶ φθάσας ἐπελάβετο, 'this word supposeth a flight of the one party, and a pursuit of the other – a pursuit eager, and so long till he overtake;' and when he hath overtaken, ἐπιλαμβανόμενος, *apprehendens*, 'laying fast hold, and seizing surely on him.' So two things it supposeth; 1, a flight of the one, and 2. a hot pursuit of the other.

It may well suppose a flight. For of the Angels there were that fled, that kept not their original, but forsook and fell away from their first estate.[1] And man fell, and fled too, and 'hid himself in the thick trees' from the presence of God.[2] And this is the first issue. Upon the Angels' flight He stirred not, sat still, never vouchsafed to follow them; let them go whither they would, as if they had not been worth the while. Nay, He never assumed aught by way of promise for them; no promise in the Old, to be born and to suffer; no Gospel in the New Testament, neither was born nor suffered for them.

---

[1] Jude 6   [2] Genesis 3:8

But when man fell He did all; made after him presently with *Ubi es?* [Where art thou?] sought to reclaim him, 'What have you done? Why have you done so?' Protested enmity to him that had drawn him thus away, made His *assumpsit* of 'the woman's seed'.[3]

And, which is more, when that would not serve, sent after him still by the hand of His Prophets, to solicit his return.

And, which is yet more, when that would not serve neither, went after him Himself in person; left His 'ninety-and-nine in the fold', and got Him after the 'lost sheep'; never left till He 'found him, laid him on His own shoulders, and brought him home again.'[4]

It was much even but to look after us, to respect us so far who were not worth the cast of His eye; much to call us back, or vouchsafe us an *Ubi es?*

But more, when we came not for all that, to send after us. For if He had but only been content to give us leave to come to Him again, but given us leave to 'lay hold' on Him, to 'touch but the hem of His garment'[5] – Himself sitting still, and never calling to us, nor sending after us – it had been favour enough, far above that we were worth. But not only to send by others, but to come Himself after us; to say, *Corpus apta Mihi, Ecce venio*; 'Get Me a body, I will Myself after Him';[6] – this was exceeding much, that we fled, and He followed us flying.

But yet this is not all, this is but to follow. He not only followed, but did it so with such eagerness, with such earnestness, as that is worthy a second consideration. To follow is somewhat, yet that may be done faintly, and afar off; but to follow through thick and thin, to follow hard and not to give over, never to give over till He overtake – that is it.

And He gave not over His pursuit, though it were long and laborious, and He full weary; though it cast Him into a 'sweat', a 'sweat of blood'.[7] *Angelis suis non pepercit*, saith St Peter, 'The Angels offending, He spared not them': man offending, He

---

3 Genesis 3:9-15
4 Luke 15:4-5
5 Matthew 9:20-21

6 Psalm 40:7
7 Luke 22:44

spared him, and to spare him, saith St Paul, 'He spared not His own Son.'[8] Nor His own Son spared not Himself, but followed His pursuit through danger, distress, yea, through death itself. Followed, and so followed, as nothing made Him leave following till He overtook.

And when He had overtaken, for those two are but pre-supposed, the more kindly to bring in the word ἐπελάβετο, [he overtook], when, I say, He had overtaken them, cometh in fitly and properly ἐπιλαμβάνεται [he seized hold of]. Which is not every 'taking', not *suscipere* or *assumere*, but *manum injicere, arri-pere, apprehendere*; 'to seize upon it with great vehemency, to lay hold on it with both hands as upon a thing we are glad we have got, and will be loath to let go again.' We know *assumpsit* and *apprehendit* both 'take;' but *apprehendit* with far more fervour and zeal than the other. *Assumpsit*, any common ordinary thing; *apprehendit*, a thing of price which we hold dear, and much esteem of.

From the Second Sermon of the Nativity, Christmas Day, 1606

Isaiah ix: 6.

For unto us a Child is born, and unto us a Son is given; and the government is upon His shoulder; and He shall call His Name Wonderful, Counsellor, the Mighty God, the Everlasting Father, the Prince of Peace.

[*Parvulus enim natus est nobis, et Filius datus est nobis, et factus est principatus super humerum ejus: et vocabitur nomen ejus, Admi-rabilis, Consiliarius, Deus, fortis, Pater futuri sæculi, Princeps Pacis.* Latin Vulg.]

---

[8] 2 Peter 2:4; Romans 8:32

[*For unto us a Child is born, unto us a Son is given, and the government shall be upon His shoulder; and His Name shall be called Wonderful, Counsellor, the Mighty God, the Everlasting Father, the Prince of Peace.* Authorized Version]

All along His Life you shall see these two. At His birth; a cratch for the Child, a star for the Son; a company of shepherds viewing the Child, a choir of Angels celebrating the Son. In His life; hungry Himself, to shew the nature of the Child; yet 'feeding five thousand', to shew the power of the Son. At His death; dying on the cross, as the 'Son of Adam'; at the same time disposing of Paradise, as the 'Son of God'.

If you ask, why both these? For that in vain had been the one without the other. Somewhat there must be borne, by this mention of shoulders; meet it is every one should bear his own burden. The nature that sinned bear his own sin; not Ziba make the fault, and Mephibosheth bear the punishment.[1] Our nature had sinned, that therefore ought to suffer; the reason, why a Child. But that which our nature should, our nature could not bear; not the weight of God's wrath due to our sin: but the Son could; the reason why a Son. The one ought but could not, the other could but ought not. Therefore, either alone would not serve; they must be joined, Child and Son. But that He was a Child, He could not have suffered. But that He was a Son, He had sunk in His suffering, and not gone through with it. God had no shoulders; man had, but too weak to sustain such a weight. Therefore, that He might be liable He was a Child, that He might be able He was the Son; that He might be both, He was both.

This, why God. But why this Person the Son? Behold 'Adam would' have 'become one of Us'[2] – the fault; behold, one of Us will become Adam, is the satisfaction. Which of Us would he have become? *Sicut Dii scientes*;[3] 'the Person of knowledge'. He therefore shall become Adam; a Son shall be given. Desire of knowledge, our attainder; He in 'Whom all the treasures of

---

[1] 2 Samuel 16:1-4, 19:24-30, 21:7   [3] Genesis 3:5
[2] Genesis 3:22

129

knowledge',[4] our restoring. Flesh would have been the Word, as wise as the Word – the cause of our ruin; meet then the 'Word become flesh',[5] that so our ruin repaired.

From the Ninth Sermon of the Nativity, Christmas Day, 1614

Isaiah vii: 14.

> *Behold, a virgin shall conceive, and bear a Son, and she shall call His name Immanuel.*

> *Ecce virgo concipiet, et pariet Filium, et vocabitur nomen Ejus Immanuel.*

> [*Behold, a virgin shall conceive, and bear a Son, and shall call His name Immanuel.* Authorized Version]

And now, to look into the name. It is compounded, and to be taken in pieces. First, into *Immanu* and *El*; of which, *El* the latter is the more principal by far; for *El* is God. Now, for any thing yet said in *concipiet* and *pariet*, all is but man with us; not 'God with us' till now. By the name we take our first notice that this Child is God. And this is a great addition, and here, lo, is the wonder. For, as for any child of a woman to 'eat butter and honey',[1] the words that next follow, where is the *Ecce*? But for *El*, for God to do it – that is worth an *Ecce* indeed.

El is God; and not God every way, but as the force of the word is, God in His full strength and virtue; God, *cum plenitudine potestatis* as we say, 'with all that ever He can do'; and that is enough I am sure.

---

[4] Colossians 2:3   [5] John 1:14

[1] Isaiah 7:15

For the other, *Immanu*; though *El* be the more principal, yet I cannot tell whether it or *Immanu* do more concern us. For as in *El* is might, so in *Immanu* is our right to His might, and to all He hath or is worth. By that word we hold, therefore we to lay hold of it. The very standing of it thus before, thus in the first place, toucheth us somewhat. The first thing ever that we look for is *nos, nobis*, and *noster*, the possessives; for they do *mittere in possessionem*, 'put us in possession'. We look for it first, and lo, it stands here first: *nobiscum* first, and then *Deus* after.

I shall not need to tell you that in *nobiscum* there is *mecum*; in *nobiscum* for us all a *mecum* for every one of us. Out of this generality of 'with us', in gross, may every one deduce his own particular – with me, and me, and me. For all put together make but *nobiscum*.

The Wise Man out of Immanuel, that is *nobiscum Deus*, doth deduce Ithiel, that is *mecum Deus*, 'God with me' – his own private interest. And St Paul when he had said to the Ephesians of Christ, 'Who loved us, and gave Himself for us', might with good right say to the Galatians, 'Who loved me and gave Himself for me.'[2]

This *Immanu* is a compound again; we may take it in sunder into *nobis* and *cum*; and so then have we three pieces. 1. *El*, the mighty God; 2. and *anu* [without], we, poor we, – poor indeed if we have all the world beside if we have not Him to be with us; 3. and *Im*, which is *cum*, and that *cum* in the midst between *nobis* and *Deus*, God and us – to couple God and us; thereby to convey the things of the one to the other. Ours to God; alas, they be not worth the speaking of. Chiefly, then, to convey to us the things of God. For that is worth the while; they are indeed worth the conveying.

This *cum* we shall never conceive to purpose, but *carendo* [without]; the value of 'with' no way so well as by without, by stripping of *cum* from *nobis*. And so let *nobis*, 'us', stand by ourselves without Him, to see what our case is but for this Immanuel; what, if this virgin's Child had not this day been born us: *nobiscum* after will be the better esteemed. For if this Child be 'Immanuel, God

---

[2] Ephesians 5:2; Galatians 2:20

with us', then without this Child, this Immanuel, we be without God. 'Without Him in this world', saith the Apostle;[3] and if without Him in this, without Him in the next; and if without Him there – if it be not *Immanu-el*, it will be *Immanu-hell*; and that and no other place will fall, I fear me, to our share. Without Him this we are. What with Him? Why, if we have Him, and God by Him, we need no more; *Immanu-el* and *Immanu-all*. All that we can desire is for us to be with Him, with God, and He to be with us; and we from Him, or He from us, never to be parted. We were with Him once before, and we were well; and when we left Him, and He no longer 'with us', then began all our misery. Whensoever we go from Him, so shall we be in evil case, and never be well till we be back with Him again.

Then, if this be our case that we cannot be without Him, no remedy then but to get a *cum* by whose means *nobis* and *Deus* may come together again. And Christ is that *Cum* to bring it to pass. The parties are God and we; and now this day He is both. God before eternally, and now to-day Man; and so both, and takes hold of both, and brings both together again. For two natures here are in Him. If conceived and born of a woman, then a man; if God with us, then God. So Esay offered his 'sign from the height above, or from the depth beneath':[4] here it is. 'From above', *El*; 'from beneath', *anu*; one of us now. And so, His sign from both. And both these natures in the unity of one Person, called by one name, even this name Immanuel.

---

[3] Ephesians 2:12

[4] Isaiah 7:11

Monday

INTRODUCTION

My voice shalt Thou hear betimes, O Lord;
early in the morning
will I direct my prayer unto Thee,
and Thou wilt look upon me.

Blessed art Thou, O Lord,
Who didst create the firmament of heaven,
the heavens and the heaven of heavens,
the heavenly powers,
Angels, Archangels, Cherubim, Seraphim.
The waters above the heavens,
mists and exhalations,
for showers, dew, hail, snow as wool,
hoar frost as ashes, ice as morsels,
clouds from the ends of the earth,
lightnings, thunders, winds out of Thy treasures,
tempests;
Waters beneath the heavens,
for drinking and for bathing.

I

CONFESSION

I will confess my sins,
and the sins of my fathers,
for I have transgressed and trespassed against
Thee, O Lord,
and walked contrary unto Thee.
Set not, O Lord, set not my misdeeds
before Thee,
nor my life in the light of Thy countenance,
but pardon the iniquity of Thy servant,
according to Thy great mercy;
as Thou hast been merciful to him from a child,
and even until now.

133

I have sinned, what shall I do unto Thee,
O Thou Preserver of men?
Why hast Thou set me as a mark against Thee,
so that I am a burden to myself?
Oh, pardon my transgression,
and take away mine iniquity.
Deliver me from going down to the pit,
for Thou hast found a ransom.

Have mercy on me, Son of David;
Lord, help me.
Yea, Lord, even the dogs eat of the crumbs
which fall from their master's table.
Have patience with me, Lord,
yet I have not wherewith to pay,
I confess to Thee;
forgive me the whole debt, I beseech Thee.

How long wilt Thou forget me, O Lord?
for ever?
How long wilt Thou hide Thy face from me?
How long shall I seek counsel in my soul,
and be so vexed in my heart day and night?
How long shall mine enemies triumph over me?
Consider and hear me, O Lord my God;
lighten mine eyes that I sleep not in death,
lest mine enemy say I have prevailed against him,
for if I be cast down, they that trouble me
will rejoice at it.
But my trust is in Thy mercy.

II

The Ten Commandments

Remove far from me
1. all iniquity and profaneness, superstition, and hypocrisy.
2. worship of idols, self-taught worship.
3. rash oath and curse.
4. neglect of or irreverence in worship.
5. pride and coldness.
6. strife and wrath.
7. lust and uncleanness.
8. indolence and fraud.
9. lying and injuriousness.
10. every evil imagination, every impure thought, every filthy desire, every unseemly thought.

Grant to me,
1. to be religious and pious.
2. to worship and serve.
3. to bless faithfully, and to swear truly.
4. to confess meetly in the congregation.
5. affection and obedience.
6. patience and good temper.
7. purity and soberness.
8. contentedness and goodness.
9. truth and incorruptness.
10. good thoughts, perseverance to the end.

III

PROFESSION

I believe in God,
1. the Father, Almighty, Maker of heaven and earth.
2. And in Jesus Christ, His Only-begotten Son, our Lord.
   (1) conceived of the Holy Ghost,
   (2) born of Mary, Ever-Virgin,

135

(3) suffered under Pontius Pilate,
(4) crucified,
(5) dead,
(6) buried,
> Who

(1) descended into hell,
(2) rose again from the dead,
(3) ascended into heaven,
(4) sat down on the right hand,
(5) to return thence,
(6) to judge both quick and dead.
3. And in the Holy Ghost,
(1) The Holy Church,
(2) Catholic,
(3) Communion of saints,
(4) Remission of sins,
(5) Resurrection of flesh,
(6) Life everlasting.

And now, Lord, what is my hope?
Truly my hope is even in Thee;
in Thee, O Lord, have I trusted,
let me never be confounded.

IV

INTERCESSION

Let us beseech God,
in behalf of the whole Creation;
for the supply of seasons,
healthy, fruitful, peaceful;
In behalf of the whole race of mankind;
for those who are not Christians;
for the conversion of Atheists, the ungodly;
Heathens, Turks, and Jews;

for all Christians;
for the restoration of all who are sick
of errors and sins;
for the confirmation of all
to whom Thou grantest truth and grace.

For the succour and comfort of all
who are dispirited, infirm, in want, unsettled,
both men and women;
For thankfulness and sobriety in all
who are cheerful, healthy, prosperous, quiet,
both men and women;
for the Catholic Church,
its establishment and increase;
for the Eastern,
its deliverance and union;
for the Western,
its renovation and peace;
for the British,
the supply of what is wanting in it,
the strengthening of what remains in it;
for the Episcopate, Presbytery, Christian laity;
for the States of the inhabited world;
for Christian states,
far off, near at hand, for our own;
for all in authority;
for our divinely-guarded King,
the Queen and the Prince;
for those who are the chief at court;
for Parliament and Judicature,
for Army and Police,
Commons and their Officers,
Farmers, Breeders of Cattle, Fishers, Merchants,
Traders, and Mechanics,
down to mean Workmen, and the Poor.

For the rising generation;
for the good nurture of all the Royal offspring,
of the scions of the Nobility;
for all in Universities, in Inns of Court,
in Schools in town or country,
in Apprenticeships.

For those who have a claim on me
from relationship,
for my Brothers and Sisters,
that God's blessing may be on them,
and on their children;

Or from benefits conferred,
that Thy recompence may be on all
who have benefited me,
who have ministered to me in carnal things;
Or from trust placed in me,
for all whom I have educated,
all whom I have ordained;
for my College, my Parish,
Southwell, St Paul's, Westminster,
dioceses of Chichester, Ely, and my present,
Clergy, Laity, Officials, Authorities,
the Deanery in the Chapel Royal,
the Almonry,
the Colleges committed to me;

Or from natural kindness,
for all who love me,
though some of them I know not;

Or from Christian love,
for those who hate me without cause,
some, too, even on account of truth and
righteousness;

Or from neighbourhood,
For all who dwell near me peacably and
harmlessly;

Or from promise,
For all whom I have promised to remember in
my prayers;
Or from mutual offices,
For all who remember me in their prayers,
and ask of me the same;

Or from stress of engagements,
For all who for reasonable causes fail to call
upon Thee;

For all who have no intercessor
in their own behalf;
For all who at present are in agony
of extreme necessity, or deep affliction;
For all who are undertaking any good work
which will bring glory to the Name of God,
or some great good to the Church;
For all who act nobly
either towards things sacred or towards the poor;
For all who have ever been offended by me
either in word or in deed.

God have mercy on me and bless me;
God shew the light of His countenance upon me
and be merciful unto me;
God, even our own God, give me His blessing,
God bless me.
Receive my prayer, O Lord;
O direct my life towards Thy commandments,
hallow my soul,
purify my body,
direct my thoughts,
cleanse my desires,

soul and body, mind and spirit, heart and reins.
Renew me thoroughly, O God,
for, if Thou wilt, Thou canst.

V
PRAISE

The Lord, the Lord God,
merciful and gracious,
long-suffering and abundant in goodness
and truth,
keeping mercy for thousands,
forgiving iniquity and transgression and sin;
that will by no means clear the guilty,
visiting the iniquity of the fathers
upon the children.

I will bless the Lord at all times,
His praise shall ever be in my mouth.
Glory to God in the highest,
and on earth peace,
goodwill towards men.

Friday

Early shall my prayer come before Thee.

Blessed are Thou, O Lord,
Who didst bring forth of the earth,
wild beasts, cattle,
and all creeping things,
for food, clothing, help;
and didst make man after Thine image,
to rule the earth,
and blessedst Him.
I would thankfully admire
the fore-counsel, fashioning hand,
breath of life, image of God,
appointment over the works,
charge to the Angels concerning him,
Paradise.
Heart, reins, eyes, ears, tongue, hands, feet;
life, sense, reason, spirit, free-will,
memory, conscience;
that which may be known of God,
the Law written in the heart,
Oracles of prophets, melody of Psalms,
instruction of Proverbs, experience of Histories,
services of Sacrifices.
Blessed art Thou, O Lord,
for Thy great and precious promise
on this day,
concerning the Life-giving Seed,
and for its fulfilment in fulness of the times
on this day.

Blessed art Thou, O Lord,
for the holy Passion
of this day.

O by Thy sufferings on this day,
for our salvation,
save us, O Lord.

I

CONFESSION

I have withstood Thee, Lord,
but I return to Thee;
for I have fallen by mine iniquity.
But I take with me words,
and I return unto Thee and say,
Take away all iniquity and receive us graciously,
so will we render the calves of our lips.
Spare us, Lord, spare
and give not Thine heritage to reproach,
to Thine enemies,

Lord, Lord, be propitious;
cease, I beseech Thee,
by whom shall Jacob arise? for he is small.
Repent, O Lord, for this, let it not be.
While observing lying vanities
I have forsaken my own mercy,
and am cast out of Thy sight.
When my soul fainted within me,
I remembered the Lord;
yet will I look again toward Thy Holy Temple;
Thou hast brought up my life from corruption.

Who is a God like unto Thee,
that pardonest iniquity
to the remnant of Thy heritage?
Thou retainest not Thine anger for ever,
because Thou delightest in mercy.

142

Turn again and have compassion upon us, O Lord,
subdue our iniquities,
and cast all our sins into the depths of the sea,
according to Thy truth, and according
to Thy mercy.

O Lord, I heard thy speech and was afraid;
I considered Thy works, and was astonished;
in wrath remember mercy.
Behold me, Lord, clothed in filthy garments;
behold Satan standing at my right hand;
yet, O Lord, by the blood of Thy covenant,
by the fountain opened for sin and for uncleanness,
take away my iniquity,
and cleanse me from my sin.

Save me as a brand
plucked out of the fire.
Father, forgive me, for I knew not,
truly I knew not, what I did
in sinning against Thee.
Lord, remember me
when Thou comest in Thy kingdom.
Lord, lay not mine enemies' sins to their charge;
Lord, lay not my own to mine.

By Thy Sweat bloody and clotted,
Thy Soul in agony,
Thy Head crowned with thorns,
bruised with staves,
Thine Eyes wet with tears,
Thine Ears full of insults,
Thy Mouth moistened with vinegar and gall,
Thy Face dishonourably stained with spitting,
Thy Neck weighed down with the burden
of the cross,
Thy Back ploughed with the wheals and gashes
of the scourge,

Thy Hands and Feet stabbed through,
Thy strong cry, Eli, Eli,
Thy Heart pierced with the spear,
the Water and Blood thence flowing,
Thy Body broken,
Thy Blood poured out,
Lord, forgive the offence of Thy servant,
and cover all his sins.
Turn away all Thy displeasure,
and turn Thyself from Thy wrathful indignation.
Turn me then, O God our Saviour,
and let Thine anger cease from us.
Wilt Thou be displeased at us for ever?
Wilt Thou stretch out Thy wrath from one
generation to another?
Wilt Thou not turn again and quicken us,
that Thy people may rejoice in Thee?
Shew us Thy mercy, O Lord,
and grant us Thy salvation.

II

PRAYER FOR GRACE

Help me to crucify the flesh and its works,
adultery, fornication,
uncleanness, lasciviousness,
idolatry, witchcraft,
enmities, strifes,
emulations, heats,
quarrels, parties,
heresies, envyings, murders,
drunkennesses, revellings, and such like.

Help me to bring forth
the fruits of the Spirit,
love, joy, peace,

long-suffering, gentleness, goodness,
faith, meekness, temperance.
Vouchsafe unto me
the spirit of wisdom, of understanding,
of counsel, of might,
of knowledge, of godliness,
of fear of the Lord.
Grant to Thy Church
the gifts of the Spirit,
the word of wisdom, of knowledge,
faith, gifts of healing, mighty works,
prophecy, discerning of spirits,
divers kinds of tongues, interpretation of tongues.
May Thy strong hand, O Lord,
be ever my defence;
Thy mercy in Christ my salvation;
Thy all-veritable word my instruction;
the grace of Thy life-bringing Spirit
my consolation
up to the end, and in the end.

May the soul of Christ hallow me,
and the Body strengthen me,
and the Blood ransom me,
and the Water wash me,
and the Bruises heal me,
and the Sweat refresh me,
and the Wound hide me.

The peace of God
which passeth all understanding,
keep my heart and my thoughts
in the knowledge and the love of God.

III

I believe
that Thou didst create me;
despise not the work of Thine own hands;
that Thou madest me after Thine own image
and likeness;
suffer not Thy likeness to be blotted out;
that Thou didst redeem me with Thy blood;
suffer not the cost of that redemption to perish;
that Thou didst call me Christian
after Thy Name;
disdain not Thine own title;
that Thou didst hallow me in regeneration;
destroy not Thy holy work;
that Thou didst graft me into the good olive-tree,
the member of a mystical body;
the member of Thy mystical body
cut not off.
O think upon Thy servant as concerning
Thy word,
wherein Thou hast caused me to put my trust.
My soul hath longed for Thy salvation,
and I have good hope because of Thy word.

IV

INTERCESSION

I pray
for the prosperous advance
and strengthening
of all the Christian army,
against the enemies of our most holy faith;
For our holy fathers,
and all our brotherhood in Christ;

For those who hate and those who love us;
For those who have mercy upon us and those
who minister to us;
For those whom we have promised
to remember in prayer;
for the liberation of captives;
For our fathers and brethren absent;
For those who voyage by sea;
For those who lie in sickness.
Let us pray also for the fruitfulness of the earth,
and for the souls of all orthodox Christians.
Let us bless pious Kings,
orthodox Prelates,
the Founders of this holy dwelling-place,
our Parents,
and all our Forefathers
and our Brethren departed.

V

PRAISE

Thou Who, on man's transgressing
Thy command, and falling,
didst not pass him by, nor leave him,
O God of goodness;
but didst visit him in ways manifold,
as a tender Father;
Supplying him with Thy great and precious
promise,
concerning the Life-giving Seed,
Opening to him the door of faith,
and of repentance unto life,
and in fulness of the times,
Sending Thy Christ Himself
to take on Him the seed of Abraham;
and, in the oblation of His Life,

to fulfil the obedience of the Law;
and, in the sacrifice of His Death,
to take away the curse of the Law;
and by His Death, to redeem the world;
and, by His Resurrection, to quicken it:
O Thou, Who doest all things,
whereby to bring back again our race to Thee,
that it may become partaker
of Thy Divine Nature and Eternal glory;
Thou, Who hast borne witness
to the truth of Thy Gospel
by many and various mighty works,
by the ever-memorable converse of Thy saints,
by their supernatural endurance of torments,
by the most wondrous conversion of
the whole world
to the obedience of faith,
without might, or rhetoric, or compulsion:
Blessed be Thy Name,
and praised, and hymned,
and magnified, and highly exalted,
and glorified, and hallowed;
its mention, and its memory,
and every memorial of it,
both now and for evermore.

Worthy art Thou to take the book,
and to open the seals thereof,
for Thou wast slain, and hast redeemed us
to God by Thy Blood,
out of every kindred, and tongue,
and people, and nation.
Worthy is the Lamb that was slain
to receive the power, and riches, and wisdom,
and strength, and honour, and glory,
and blessing.

To Him that sitteth upon the throne,
and to the Lamb,
be the blessing, and the honour, and the glory,
and the might,
for ever and ever. Amen.
Salvation to our God, Which sitteth upon
the throne, and to the Lamb.
Amen.
They blessing and the glory and the
wisdom,
and the thanksgiving and the honour,
and the power and the strength,
be unto our God,
for ever and ever,
Amen.

An Act of Thanksgiving

1. The Excellence of God's Majesty.
Glorify Thou Me, O Father,
with Thine own self,
with the glory which I had with Thee before
the world was.
Melchizedek was Priest of the Most High God.

2. His Exaltedness.
He that is higher than the highest regardeth.

3. His Eternity.
The Lord, the everlasting God.

4. His Omnipresence.
Do I not fill Heaven and earth? saith the Lord.

5. His Omniscience.
Whither shall I go then from Thy Spirit?
or whither shall I go from Thy Presence?
If I climb up into Heaven, Thou art there;
if I go down into Hell, Thou art there also.
Thou knowest all things.
For Thou only knowest the hearts of the
children of men.

6. His Omnipotence.
With God nothing shall be impossible.
I am the Almighty God.

7. The Height of His Wisdom
O the depth of the riches of the wisdom and
knowledge of God;
how unsearchable are His judgments!
and His ways past finding out!

8. His Unshaken Truth.

The truth of the Lord endureth forever,
Heaven and earth shall pass away,
but My words shall not pass away.

9. His Exquisite Justice.

His Justice endureth for ever.

10. The Fountain, Ocean, Abyss of His Mercy.

Deep calleth unto deep.

11. He is Merciful in Passing by and
Overlooking Sin.

I beseech you by the meekness and gentleness
of Christ.
I will not destroy it for ten's sake.
He passeth by transgressions.
The times of ignorance God winked at.

12. He is Patient, Long-suffering.

Or despisest Thou the riches of His forbearance,
and long-suffering?

13. Pitiful.

But He was so merciful, that He forgave
their misdeeds,
and destroyed them not.

14. He Punisheth Unwillingly.

O Ephraim, what shall I do unto thee?
O Judah, what shall I do unto thee?
Yet many years didst Thou forbear them;
for Thy great mercies' sake
Thou didst not utterly consume them,
nor forsake them.
He doth not deal with us after our sins,
neither rewardeth us according to our iniquities.

She hath received of the Lord's hand
double for all her sins.
Like as a father pitieth his own children,
even so is the Lord merciful unto them that
fear Him.

15. Compassionate.
He repenteth Him of the evil.

16. His Anger is Soon Quenched.
He will not always be chiding,
neither keepeth He His anger for ever.

17. He is Ready to Pardon.
I forgave thee all that debt, because thou
desiredst Me.

18. Ready to be Reconciled.
Reconciling the world unto Himself,
not imputing their trespasses unto them.

19. Ready to be Propitiated.
Bring forth the best robe, and put it on him;
and put a ring on his hand,
and shoes on his feet.
He is good and kind to the unthankful and
to the evil.

20. Munificent.
Giving the reward of a day for the toil of an hour.
'To-day shalt thou be with Me in Paradise.'

Giving sight to the blind,	loosing the bound,
clothing the naked,	raising the fallen,
upholding the falling,	healing the sick,
gathering the dispersed,	feeding the living,
sustaining the hungry,	quickening the dead,
casting down the proud,	setting up the humble,
redeeming the captives,	helping in time of need.

Who is like unto Thee, O Lord, among the Gods?
glorious in holiness, fearful in praises,
doing wonders?

Let us praise God for
Angels, the guardians of men;
Archangels, announcing, by their illumination,
mightier events;
the voice of the Archangel:
Virtues, that do wonders;
Angels, authorities, and powers being made
subject unto Him.
Powers, that ward off evil spirits,
at His command:
Principalities, perfect in government;
Dominations, that bestow gifts in plenteousness;
Thrones, that judge at the tribunal;
whether they be thrones, or dominions,
or principalities, or powers,
all things were created by Him and for Him.
Cherubim brilliant with knowledge;
He placed Cherubim before Paradise;
Seraphim, burning with love;
above it stood the Seraphim:
each one had six wings.
The morning stars,
rulers of the world,
lovers of men,
chief ministers of the Divine Will;
we laud God for the perseverance of Angels;
we pray that we, going from strength to strength,
may be associated with their choirs.

We praise Him for
The Patriarchs and their faith,
The Prophets and their hope,
The Apostles and their labours,
The Evangelists and their truth,

153

The Martyrs and their blood,
The Confessors and their zeal,
The Doctors and their study,
The Asceticks and their tears,
The Virgins, flowers of purity,
celestial gems,
brides of the Immaculate Lamb;
The Innocents and their beauty,
flowers of the Church,
mirrors of virtue,
tabernacles of the Holy Ghost.
For those, whose faith was strong, and whose
life approved;
in whose heart was charity,
in whose mouth verity,
in whose life piety.

We praise Him for
light,
the waters and the Heaven,
the earth and the plants,
the luminaries,
the fishes and the fowls,
the wild and tame beasts,
the rest of the Sabbath.
For the formation of man,
after counsel held,
with His Own hands,
with the breath of life,
in the Image of God,
for the dominion over the creatures,
the care of Angels,
the placing in Paradise,
that he was not forsaken, when he had sinned.

For the Promise of the Seed of the woman,
that which may be known of God,
the work of the Law written in the heart,

the oracles of the Prophets,
the melody of the Psalms,
the wisdom of the Proverbs,
the experience of the Histories.

Come, Holy Ghost, our souls inspire,
And lighten with celestial fire;
Thou the Anointing Spirit art,
Who dost Thy sevenfold gifts impart.

We would thankfully commemorate,
in the Old Testament,
(1) Thy moving upon the face of the waters,
(2) Thy sending forth into all things living,
(3) Thy Inspiration of man,
of Bezaleel,
of the Seventy Elders,
(4) Thy descent upon the Prophets.

Thy Visible Advent

(1) As a shadow;
Thy coming upon and overshadowing
the Blessed Virgin
at the Conception of Christ.

(2) As a dove;
Thy coming in the shape of a dove
upon Christ in Baptism.

(3) As breath;
Thy coming upon the Apostles
in the breath of Christ
after the Resurrection.

155

(4) As fiery tongues;
      Thy sitting upon the Apostles
        in fiery tongues
        after the Ascension:

Thy Invisible Advent

(1) on the Apostles gathered together in prayer,
(2) on Cornelius,
(3) on the twelve Ephesians.
      Thy often visitations thenceforth;
      In calling;
(1) calling away from sin;
(2) calling out of the world,
(3) recalling from backsliding;
(4) In our calling on Thee;
      in Thy pleading for us.
      Thy diversities of Graces, Ministrations,
        Operations,
      The gifts of the Spirit; Works, Fruits.
(1) The compunction caused by Thy conviction,
(2) the unction of Thy Teaching,
(3) Thy bringing to remembrance,
(4) Thy shedding forth of Love,
(5) Thy helping our infirmities in prayer,
(6) Thy witnessing to our Adoption,
(7) Thy Sealing in Thy mysteries,
(8) the Earnest of our Inheritance.

    (1) Thy visiting us to visit the heart,
    (2) Thy dwelling in us,
    (3) Thy purifying of us,
    (4) Thy shining on us, to enlighten us,
    (5) Thy strengthening us,
    (6) Thy adorning us,
    (7) Thy leading us to perfection;
        As the Guide unto all truth,
          the Supplier of strength.

156

We give Thee thanks
for the Triumph of Mercy,
through and for Thy Name's Sake,
the glory of Thy Name,
the truth of Thy Promise,
the confirmation by Thine Oath,
the comfort of Love,
bowels of mercies.
Thy Mercy which is manifold,
great, even of old, plenteous,
everlasting, exceeding, marvellous;
the riches of Thy Mercy,
its superabundance, its exceeding riches,
its victory over all Thy works,
over justice,
the satisfaction and merits of Christ,
the consolation of the Holy Ghost.

THANKSGIVING FOR GOD'S MERCY

We give Thee thanks
for Thy Mercy
that we are not consumed,
that preventeth, followeth, surroundeth,
forgiveth, crowneth;
for its length, breadth, depth, height;
that it is from everlasting to everlasting,
reacheth to Heaven, reacheth to hell,
is over all,
is tender, sweet, better than life;
as is Thy Majesty,
pardoning unto seventy times seven,
hating nothing that it hath made,
neglecting neither the young ravens,
nor the sparrows,
willing that all men should be saved,

not willing that any should perish,
bringing back the lost sheep on the shoulder,
sweeping the house for the piece of silver,
forgiving the ten thousand talents,
binding up the wounds of the half-dead,
joyfully meeting the Prodigal Son,
freeing the fugitive Jonah,
receiving the denying Peter,
not rejecting the incredulous Thomas,
converting the blaspheming Saul,
letting go the woman taken in adultery,
receiving Mary Magdalene,
opening Paradise to the thief,
standing at the door and knocking,
the Lord Himself entreating His own servants,
Thou, whose place is the Throne of Grace,
the Mercy-seat,
whose time is the Day of Salvation.

I have deferred repentance,
and Thou hast prolonged patience,
O Thou that art Mercy,
Thou that art a Fountain inexhaustible!